Broken Border

Understanding the Global Forces Shaping the Immigration Crisis

TIM TROTT

TIM TROTT

Book Cover Design by Tim Trott and Daim Atiq, assisted by MidJourney Ai.
The cover image is not a realistic representation, but a visualization of a common conception.

Revision 20 – April 9, 2024

I want to express my appreciation and acknowledgment to those special unnamed people who provided their input and personal perspectives to my research on this complex topic.

Contents

Foreword   1

Introduction   3

The Crossing   5

The History   9

The People   21

The Motivation   27

The Forces   33

The Numbers   37

The Path to the Border   43

The Barriers   57

The Objections   67

Breaking the Myths   71

The Root Causes   75

Counterproductive Measures   85

Who Gets It Right?   89

What Does Mexico Do?   95

Possible Solutions   103

The Way Forward 117

References and Resources 119

About the Author 123

Foreword

"I certainly approve of your aspirations and fact-based analysis in general. (It seems to have fallen out of fashion.) Most people are relying on their preconceptions and misconceptions instead. In particular, border policy has become more of a metaphor than an issue to be resolved with knowledge, wisdom, and a good heart."

Alan Grayson, attorney, former representative.
"The Congressman with Guts"
Member U.S. House of Representatives, 9th District, Florida, 2013-2017

Introduction

I t could be said that everyone agrees there is a problem with the borders, but nobody agrees about how to solve it. Not only is there disagreement as to how to manage the borders, but there is no real consensus as to an effective approach, or even as to the full extent of the issue. And that disagreement can be found on both sides of the border. There are even some factions who don't want it solved.

The current situation is marked by heightened attention to border security with a related concern about what to do with migrants already in the country. As the United States navigates this intricate landscape, the discussion on illegal immigration continues to unfold against a backdrop of shifting dynamics, emphasizing the need for comprehensive and collaborative solutions that balance enforcement with humanitarian considerations and address the root causes driving migration.

This book is the result of research compiled from a number of resources, including immigrant interviews, books, online searches, YouTube videos as well as several Artificial Intelligence functions. Let it be said that the issues surrounding immigration are wide-ranging. The varied elements forming the current crisis stretch back decades and centuries, across complex issues and history.

There are no simple answers. The only agenda you will find in this book is an effort to shed light on all the hidden corners inside the box. To that point, if anyone had the answer, it would have been solved by now. No matter which side of the political or border fence you happen to be on, be prepared to have your assumptions shattered.

This book attempts to present the Big Picture of international immigration challenges.

We begin by inviting you to envision a border crossing from the migrant's perspective.

The Crossing

A Crossing Story:

The icy sting of the Rio Grande sliced through Esperanza's worn boots, biting at her ankles like a hungry coyote. Her breath puffed white against the velvet darkness, each exhalation a prayer whispered into the January night. Beside her, Miguel, her ten-year-old son, shivered and clutched his threadbare sweater tighter. Luna, Esperanza's eight-year-old daughter, held tightly to her hand.

"Mamá," Luna whimpered, "Está muy frío." [I'm very cold]

Esperanza's heart ached, a dull thrumming against the icy water. "Shhh, mi luna," she soothed, her voice rough with emotion. "Casi estamos." [We're almost there]

The river bank on the American side loomed ahead, a shadowy silhouette against the dark sky. Beyond it lay a better life. Here, in the barren fields of Mexico, their bellies growled with hunger, their nights were haunted by the hollow echoes of empty promises. America, they were told, was a land of plenty, a shimmering oasis where dreams bloomed like desert flowers.

But the Rio Grande, a churning serpent guarding the promised land, snarled its protest. The current tugged at their ankles, a silent threat of its swift, icy depths. Esperanza tightened her grip on Luna's hand, her palm slick with a cold sweat born not just of the water, but of fear.

"Miguelito," [Little Miguel] she whispered, "Ve primero. Ten cuidado con las rocas." [Go first. Be careful of the rocks]

Miguel, small but wiry, nodded and stepped into the water. He waded cautiously, his bare feet sending ripples that shimmered under the moon. Luna, her chin tucked into Esperanza's shoulder, watched with wide eyes. The current tugged at Miguel, but he fought it, showing courage beyond his young age.

Now it was her chance. She picked up Luna and held her tight. With a deep breath, she stepped into the water. The current tugged at her legs, soon throwing her off balance. A gasp slipped out, but she clenched her teeth, holding Luna more tightly. The cold water soaked through her old dress, sending a chill to her core. She persisted, each step a struggle against the river's icy grasp. In the faint light, Esperanza saw the opposite bank of the river. She pressed on.

Now gasping for breath in the swirling current, she tried without success to hold her young daughter above the cold water. Splashing sounds and cries ahead told her Miguel was also struggling to stay above the cold waves. Then at once, before she could even gasp, cold water filled her lungs in a rush. She lost her grip on Luna, and as if by invisible strings, the river pulled her down.

In a moment, it was over. After a time, figures with flashlights emerged from the shore in a small boat from the Mexican side, eventually locating the now lifeless bodies of the mother and her two children.

***

The Reality:

What you have just experienced is pure fiction, but it could be what happened to 33 year old Victerma de la Sancha Cerros, a Mexican citizen, who tried unsuccessfully to cross the Rio Grande near Eagle Pass, Texas, with her two children. Yorlei Rubi was ten and Johnathan Agustin Briones de la Snacha was eight, as later confirmed by Mexico's National Institute of Migration. That happened in mid January of 2024.

While they might not have been able to save the woman and her two children, the Border Patrol asserted in a sworn statement that Texas soldiers blocked their agents from reaching two other migrants who were also in distress.

Texas National Guard came under criticism for blocking the U.S. Border Patrol from that section of the border. The area includes Shelby Park, a city park on the Rio Grande that Texas authorities blocked off with fencing, gates, and razor wire – effectively denying access to federal agents.

The border is technically federal land, which is under the jurisdiction of the U.S. Border Patrol. However, Texas refused to allow the Border Patrol to park along the U.S.-Mexico border at Shelby Park in Eagle Pass on the Rio Grande. The Border Patrol confirms that they have been denied access to the area even in emergency situations.[1]

Negative comments to YouTube coverage of the event included some who said things like, "It's their own damn fault for trying to illegally enter

---

1. https://www.latimes.com/world-nation/story/2024-01-17/texas-border-access-migrants-drowning-what-we-know

other countries" or " They should have stayed home; no one invited them here." Other comments were more compassionate.

The question remains, what would drive a woman to take that kind of chance with the lives of her children? How desperate would she have to be? How could she be convinced that she could succeed? In this particular case, we don't know the woman's background or her motives. Her sister, who was able to cross, could have provided some hint, if anyone thought to ask. Beyond that, we an only guess.

We do know that she was a Mexican citizen. Was she under threat by the drug cartels? Was she trying to join her husband or relatives in the United States? Was her husband killed or captured by the drug cartels forcing her to leave her country? Were the drug cartels demanding monthly payments to stay where she lived? Any of these are possible.

And yet, the pattern repeats thousands of times, not just with Mexican citizens, but for others, often braving the long and treacherous path from South America through the jungles and swamps of Panama, Costa Rica, Nicaragua, Honduras and Guatemala, even indirectly from Cuba. Others take flights directly to Mexico or other Central American countries with relatively lax immigration policies and continue their journey from there.

To many of us, border security may be a fairly recent concern, brought to our attention through news and political speeches. But the history of migration goes back to the very beginning. The United States, of course, was founded by immigrants. For the first hundred years, immigration was a normal part of life.

When we hear numbers like 11 million "illegal immigrants" in the United States, keep in mind, that number is likely only an approximation of first-generation immigrants that we have any way of knowing about.

To fully understand the scope of the issue, we need to take into account the history of migration in the United States.

The History

The influx of migrants to the United States has been influenced by several historic national and international factors throughout history.

The history of the United States is a history of immigration, as the earliest waves of immigrants to the American colonies were driven by European settlers. Puritans, Quakers and Catholics established colonies with distinct religious and cultural identities.

Early settlers came to the U.S. seeking religious freedom, escaping persecution in Europe. This trend continued with various religious groups seeking refuge over the centuries. Political instability and persecution in home countries have driven waves of immigrants to the U.S. For example, refugees from conflicts in Southeast Asia, Central America, and the Middle East sought asylum in the U.S. People from Ireland came to the U.S. seeking escape from the Great Famine between 1845 and 1852.

World War I saw a temporary decline in immigration due to the disruption of transatlantic travel. The passage of the Immigration Act of 1924 was a result of increasing anti-immigrant sentiments in the country and strict quotas were imposed.

The Industrial Revolution in the 19th century led to economic changes and job opportunities in the United States, attracting European immigrants seeking better economic prospects. During the early to mid-20th century, the U.S. experienced economic growth, particularly after World War II. This prosperity attracted migrants from Europe, Asia, and Latin America in search of employment and improved living standards.

Displaced persons and refugees after World War II contributed to a significant wave of immigration to the U.S., including Holocaust survivors and those fleeing communist regimes.

The Cold War period continued from the end of the second world war into the early 1990s. During that time, the U.S. sought to demonstrate the attractiveness of the American system of government, welcoming immigrants who could contribute to the economic and technological advancement of the nation's economy. The Immigration and Nationality Act of 1965 replaced earlier immigration quotas based on national origin, leading to increased immigration from Asia, Africa, and Latin America. The Vietnam War and its aftermath led to a large influx of Vietnamese refugees in the 1970s. Legislation, such as the Refugee Act of 1980, provided a framework for the admission of refugees, contributing to increased migration from regions facing humanitarian crises.

Economic disparities between developed and developing countries have motivated people to seek better economic opportunities in the United States. Advances in transportation and communication have made it easier for people to migrate and stay connected with their home countries, contributing to increased international migration.

Climate change, natural disasters, and environmental degradation can displace communities, leading to migration in search of more sustainable living conditions. Family reunification policies have played a significant role in immigration patterns, as individuals often migrate to join family members who have already settled in the U.S. This practice is often referred to as "chain migration." A recent president criticized the use of "chain migration" but that very process was used to facilitate entry of the family of that president's wife. I'll let the reader do the research on that case.

Understanding the historical context of immigration to the United States involves considering these complex and interconnected factors. Immigration patterns have evolved over time, shaped by a combination of economic, political, social, and environmental forces on a global scale. In the early 1900s, border crossings were not considered a serious problem in the United States. Relatively free movement across the U.S.–Mexican border was a benefit to Southern farmers. Chinese labor was used to expand the western railroads. Migration was a convenient answer to the need for cheap labor.

The history of immigration on the southern border paints a picture of a continuous interplay of economic, political, and social factors, with policy changes responding to evolving circumstances and priorities. That was until the Border Patrol was created in 1924. Under the Republican administration of President Calvin Coolidge, the Patrol's job was to control unauthorized immigration. The primary focus was on preventing Chinese immigrants from entering the U.S.

The Monroe Doctrine (1823)

The implementation of the Monroe Doctrine, initially intended to prevent European colonization, frequently resulted in American interventions in Latin American countries. These interventions, sometimes controversial, influenced political instability and economic conditions in the region, contributing to factors that drive migration from these countries to the United States. Immigrants who are educated in the history of South

America and Cuba consider the Monroe Doctrine as an important piece of the immigration puzzle. Many migrants point to the Monroe Doctrine as one of the factors behind increasing migration away from those countries.

Throughout history, the United States has used the Monroe Doctrine to justify its intervention and interference in the governments of Cuba, Central America, and South America.

The United States intervened in Cuba multiple times in the late 19th and early 20th centuries, citing the Monroe Doctrine as justification. This included the Spanish-American War in 1898, where the U.S. supported Cuban rebels in their fight against Spanish colonial rule. After the war, the U.S. occupied Cuba until 1902 and maintained a significant influence over its affairs. The doctrine was invoked to justify U.S. interventions in Cuban politics during the 20th century, including support for authoritarian regimes like that of Fulgencio Batista.

The U.S. used the Monroe Doctrine to justify interventions in several Central American countries during the early 20th century. For example, in Nicaragua, the U.S. intervened multiple times between 1909 and 1933 to protect American business interests and prevent the establishment of governments perceived as unfriendly to U.S. interests. This included occupations, military interventions, and support for various regimes favorable to American corporations.

The U.S. has also used the Monroe Doctrine as a justification for its intervention in South American countries. One notable example is the U.S. involvement in Chile during the early 1970s. The Nixon administration, concerned about the rise of socialist Salvador Allende to the presidency, supported efforts to destabilize his government. This culminated in the 1973 coup d'état led by General Augusto Pinochet, which overthrew Allende's government and installed a military dictatorship. Critics widely condemn the U.S. for its role in supporting the coup, with some arguing that it was justified under the Monroe Doctrine's principle of preventing the spread of communism in the Western Hemisphere.

Bracero Program (1942-1964)

Sentiment shifted in the opposite direction in 1942 under the Democratic administration of Franklin D. Roosevelt. A severe labor shortage during World War II presented a need for bringing in temporary agricultural workers from Mexico. Once the crops were harvested, most of the temporary workers went back to Mexico. The border crossing was fairly easy.

Support from a Democratic majority in Congress resulted in the creation of the Bracero Program [1]. Farmers benefited, Americans had food on the table, and there was enough to feed the troops overseas.

Operation Wetback (1954)

That policy changed when Republicans controlled the White House and Congress in 1954 with the launch of "Operation Wetback[2]." The change in policy was in response to concerns over undocumented immigration, while opposition cited the program's harsh methods and abuse of human rights. Sound familiar?

---

1. https://guides.loc.gov/latinx-civil-rights/bracero-program

2. https://www.britannica.com/topic/Operation-Wetback

As a result of increased border security, millions of migrant workers were trapped, unable to return to Mexico. That meant "undocumented" workers had to find other jobs during the off-season. Some of them had children who were born in this country.

While Democrats were in control of both houses of Congress in 1986, Republican President Ronald Reagan ran for a second term in office. Reagan's second term campaign was aimed at Immigration Reform, and the cycle continued.

Immigration Reform and Control Act (IRCA) 1986

While it resulted in increased border enforcement, the IRCA[3] was a compromise. It granted amnesty to certain undocumented immigrants, but it also established penalties for employers hiring unauthorized workers. That delicate balance remained until the election of Democratic president Bill Clinton.

North American Free Trade Agreement (NAFTA) 1994

---

3. https://guides.loc.gov/latinx-civil-rights/irca

NAFTA[4] was intended to reduce the incentive for migration by improving economic conditions in Mexico. It failed to achieve that goal. The agreement faced criticism for contributing rather than relieving economic disparities.

The 1990s and early 2000s saw a significant increase[5] in border enforcement measures, including the construction of barriers and the deployment of additional Border Patrol agents.

Secure Fence Act (2006)

Republicans elected George W. Bush and held a slim majority in congress in 2001. Construction of physical barriers along the U.S.-Mexico border began with the Secure Fence Act[6]. The debate continues as to the effectiveness of the barriers in deterring unauthorized migration.

Meanwhile, a generation of children of migrant workers who could not return to their home country were becoming adults. Now, two decades later, these children face the dual challenge of supporting themselves while

---

4. https://www.uscis.gov/working-in-the-united-states/temporary-workers/tn-nafta-professionals

5. https://www.migrationpolicy.org/article/immigration-enforcement-spending-rising

6. https://www.congress.gov/109/plaws/publ367/PLAW-109publ367.pdf

avoiding deportation to a country where, having grown up in the United States, they did not even speak the same language.

Deferred Action for Childhood Arrivals (DACA) 2012

With Democrats regaining control of the White House, the Obama administration introduced DACA[7] . The program provided temporary relief from deportation and work authorization for certain undocumented individuals brought to the U.S. as children. In many cases, those children knew nothing of their country of origin, let alone any understanding of the language. Their roots and all their experience was in this country.

Zero Tolerance Policy (2018)

After the 2016 election, the Trump administration implemented a "Zero Tolerance[8] " policy. The result was the disorganized separation of families at the border, along with widespread condemnation and legal challenges. Because of either incompetence or intention, or a combination of both, the implementation resulted in thousands of immigrant children being placed in shelters or placed in (paid) foster care. President Trump's senior adviser, Stephen Miller, and other administration officials promot-

---

7. https://www.usa.gov/daca

8. https://sgp.fas.org/crs/homesec/R45266.pdf

ed the harsh family separation policy as an aggressive deterrent, hoping it would discourage immigration across the border. Indications are that over 5,500 migrant children became separated from parents at the southwest border.

The resulting mess has little hope of ever being cleaned up, placing further burdens on the system resources. Available figures show that of the thousands separated in 2018, hundreds remained apart from parents years later because of the incomplete documentation of deportations complicated the reunification processes. The Trump administration's many changes to immigration policies also created an environment of uncertainty. Rapid changes in policies, especially related to asylum, may have inadvertently lead to increased migration as individuals sought to enter the U.S. before facing potential policy shifts. The incentive had the opposite effect of what was intended.

The Biden administration attempted to untangle the mess with the creation of the *Family Reunification Task Force*[9] in February of 2021 (see below).

Migrant Protection Protocols (MPP) 2019

---

9. https://www.dhs.gov/family-reunification-task-force

The MPP[10], also known as the "Remain in Mexico"[11] policy, created under the Trump administration, required certain asylum seekers to be sent back to Mexico to await immigration proceedings. This policy aimed to address challenges related to asylum processing. The problem is, the "temporary" wait can often last for years or decades. Under Mexican law, migrants from countries other than Mexico find it difficult to obtain employment or visas. The result is an incentive to cross back over the border into the United States, where enforcement of labor laws remains conveniently underfunded. The Biden administration attempted to reverse Trump-era policies by ending MPP and trying to reunite separated families. With a series of executive orders, the Biden administration created the *Family Reunification Task Force,* aimed at addressing immigration challenges. The goal was to reunite families separated under the Trump administration's "zero tolerance" policy. Unfortunately, records from the previous administration were incomplete or did not exist. Meanwhile, the situation was complicated by increasing numbers of migrants at the border.

MPP didn't work under Trump, and the subsequent Biden Administration went to court to overturn it. [12] That lasted only a few months until a Texas judge put a stop to it. [13]

---

10. https://www.dhs.gov/news/2019/01/24/migrant-protection-protocols

11. https://www.hrw.org/tag/remain-mexico

The "Remain in Mexico" solution was fraught with practical obstacles. The biggest question was, who pays the bills? Another problem with that policy is that it conflicted with the policy of the Mexican government. Mexico has rejected any attempt to reinstate the policy. [14]

Republicans in Congress demand enforcement on the border. Enforcement requires manpower, specifically border agents. Spending cuts voted by Congress resulted in the loss of 2,000 positions in the border patrol and related positions reinforcing the border. For that reason, Republicans have been accused of undermining and weakening border enforcement in order to maintain a campaign issue.

The system is not just overloaded, it is overwhelmed. Deporting people who have entered the country illegally requires processing. Limiting or reducing the staffing of the agency that processes deportation creates a backlog. The longer the backlog, the worse the problem gets. The worse the problem gets, the lower the prospects of being deported and thus the greater the incentive to cross the border.

See how that works?

You may now begin to see the complexity of the issue.

There is no "magic button" to make it all go away. And we are not alone. The reality is that the border issues facing the United States are not unique. Similar situations exist in many other countries around the world.

If any other countries could find a solution, we might gain by their example. But there are no good examples to follow. In Europe, there are concerns over irregular migration from Northern Africa and the Middle East. The war in Ukraine has generated refugees fleeing to Poland and

---

14. https://abcnews.go.com/Politics/mexico-rejects-effort-reinstate-rem ain-mexico-policy-asylum/story?id=96939554

Romania. The exit of the United Kingdom from the European Union (BREXIT) has created problems and trade friction with neighboring Ireland. Colombia and Venezuela have issues with migration, drug traffic, and migration resulting from ongoing political turmoil in Venezuela. The Amazon rainforest sees increasing cross-border issues with illegal logging and illegal trafficking in wildlife.

In Africa, the activity of militant groups contributes to instability at the borders of countries like Mali and Niger. Similar issues have triggered a refugee flow from Somalia and South Sudan. Ethnic tension and armed conflict has fueled displacement along on the borders of the Democratic Republic of the Congo and Burundi.

Asia is not immune to migration and border issues in the mountains of Tajikistan and Kyrgyzstan. Border resources and infrastructure are strained at the border between Myanmar and Bangladesh. Ongoing territorial disputes and security concerns maintain tensions in the South China Sea. Even Canada has expressed increasing concerns about their border with the United States.

The fact is, nobody has good answers.

To gain a better perspective of the problem, we need to understand the people and the motivations of those people who decide to leave their native country and the motives behind that decision.

The People

To understand the dimensions of the problem we must first define the components of the issue. Those who wish to enter a country are divided among three groups. Each is a separate group with distinct motivations.

Migrant:

Migration is a global phenomenon with historical, economic, and social drivers. It has significant implications for societies, economies, and the well-being of individuals and communities. A migrant is someone who moves from one country to another for various reasons, like wanting a better life, job opportunities, or a brighter future. The term "migrant" is used in this context to describe people who leave their home countries for reasons other than war, persecution, or violence.

Migrants are individuals who move from one place to another, whether within a country or across international borders. The term encompasses various types of movement, including economic migration, forced migration, and seasonal migration.

Migrants include a diverse group, such as economic migrants seeking better job opportunities, refugees fleeing persecution or conflict, internally displaced persons (IDPs) moving within their own country, and seasonal workers.

Migrants may have different legal statuses, ranging from those with proper documentation to undocumented or irregular migrants. Unlike immigrants, migrants may not necessarily have the intention of settling permanently in the destination. The movement can be temporary or circular. At one time, southern farmers, particularly those in Georgia, came to rely on temporary workers for harvesting crops. When the borders were closed, those workers found themselves trapped. So, some of them stayed. When children were born, those children became U.S. citizens, adding another layer of complexity to the problem. Others were prevented from returning from Mexico and the next harvest rotted in the fields, resulting in huge losses for farmers.

Immigrant:

An immigrant is an individual who has moved to a different country and has established residency, whether legally or illegally. The term "immigrant" is commonly used to refer to people who have permanently settled in a new country. There is overlap between the two terms, and a person can be both an immigrant and a migrant at different points in their life. For example, someone might initially move for work opportunities (as a migrant) but later decide to settle permanently (becoming an immigrant).

The context in which these terms are used can vary. Discussions about immigration often focus on policies related to individuals moving across international borders, while migration encompasses broader patterns of movement.

Understanding the distinctions between immigrants and migrants helps frame discussions around the diverse reasons for human movement and the different experiences of individuals based on their intentions and circumstances.

Asylum Seeker:

An asylum seeker is someone who has left their home country and is seeking international protection from dangers like war, violence, or persecution. Asylum seekers need to apply for protection in the country they are heading to and must prove that they meet the criteria to be recognized as refugees. It's important to note that not every asylum seeker will be granted refugee status.

Asylum seekers are individuals who have fled their home countries due to fear of persecution based on factors such as race, religion, nationality, political opinion, or membership in a particular social group. Cuban refugees fit that description.

It's crucial to recognize the complexity of the asylum process and the various factors that influence the experiences of undocumented asylum seekers. Public discourse often involves discussions about border security, the humanitarian aspects of asylum, and the need for comprehensive immigration reform.

Processing for each of these groups is different conditioned upon both their legal status and rights. A migrant may be seeking temporary employment, such as was the case with the farm workers in Georgia and elsewhere in the early part of the last century. Asylum Seekers carry with them a certain amount of urgency due to the real or imagined dangers they may have faced in their country of origin. The last group comprises those seeking escape from poverty or environmental conditions in their home country. Individual circumstances determine the legal process for each situation.

When discussing asylum seekers in the context of undocumented immigration, it's important to understand the legal framework surrounding asylum. The right to seek asylum is recognized under international law, including the 1951 Refugee Convention and its 1967 Protocol. These agreements outline the obligations of states to protect refugees and not return them to countries where they may face persecution.

In the United States, individuals can apply for asylum if they meet the criteria outlined in immigration law. The application process involves proving a well-founded fear of persecution on the basis of the aforementioned factors. Asylum seekers may arrive with or without proper documentation, and their cases are considered on an individual basis. Some asylum seekers may enter a country without proper documentation, often due to the urgency of their situation or challenges in obtaining travel documents. Once in the host country, they can express their intention to seek asylum, and the legal process begins. In some cases, undocumented asylum seekers may be detained by immigration authorities while their cases are processed. Others may be released into the community, often with certain conditions such as wearing an ankle monitor or periodic check-ins with immigration authorities. However, transporting these immigrants to the far reaches of the country for political motives can prevent them from complying with those requirements.

The issue of undocumented immigration, including the arrival of asylum seekers without proper documentation, is a contentious topic. Debates often center around national security concerns, humanitarian considerations, and the capacity of the immigration system to process cases efficiently. Immigration policies, including those related to asylum, can change over time based on government decisions and legislative changes. Changes in administration may bring about shifts in how asylum cases are handled and the treatment of undocumented asylum seekers.

The message to potential immigrants might be "go now, it could get worse."

The plain fact is that the U.S. economy relies on immigrant labor, both legal and illegal. Crops were left in the fields in Georgia in recent times due to a diminished supply of migrant labor following the state's crackdown on illegal immigration. Food processing factories traditionally employ large numbers of immigrants.

In 2011, Georgia's agriculture commissioner testified that a farm labor shortage resulting from a law targeting illegal immigration led to crops such as watermelons, onions, blueberries, and blackberries being left unharvested and rotting in the fields [1]. The shortage of about 11,000 workers caused significant agricultural losses, with some farmers losing tens of millions of dollars. Despite high unemployment in the state, local workers were not willing to take up the back-breaking and low-paying jobs typically done by migrant workers, leading to a significant impact on the agricultural industry.[2]

The state's economy suffered as a result of driving away needed workers, and some farmers were forced to reduce the planting of crops or stop

---

1. https://www.al.com/wire/2011/10/crackdown_on_illegal_immigrant.html

2. https://www.forbes.com/sites/realspin/2012/05/17/the-law-of-unintended-consequences-georgias-immigration-law-backfires/

planting altogether due to the lack of labor. The impact was felt across various crops that require hand harvesting, such as peas, cantaloupes, watermelons, onions, peppers, and cucumbers.

To understand the scope of the issue we need to study the motivation that drives people to leave their home country.

The Motivation

Various factors can influence the decision to seek entry into the United States, and individual motivations can vary. Undocumented immigrants often migrate in search of better economic opportunities. They may believe that the U.S. offers improved job prospects, higher wages, and overall better living standards compared to their home countries, including Mexico. Many Americans assume that is the only motivation, and for many, it is that simple, but for others, there can be any of many reasons.

Family Reunification: Many immigrants are motivated by the desire to reunite with family members who are already living in the United States. Family ties and the hope for a better life for the entire family unit play a significant role.

Safety and Security: Individuals fleeing violence, persecution, or insecurity in their home countries may see the United States as a safer destination. Seeking refuge from conflict, political instability, or human rights abuses is a non-economic motivation for migration.

Asylum and Protection: Some immigrants seek asylum in the United States out of fear of persecution based on factors such as race, religion, nationality, political opinion, or membership in a particular social group. They are motivated by the need for protection and humanitarian assistance.

Educational Opportunities: For some migrants, access to quality education is a significant motivator. They may seek opportunities for themselves or their children to pursue higher education and academic advancement in the United States.

Healthcare Access: Individuals facing limited access to healthcare in their home countries may migrate to the U.S. in search of better medical facilities, treatments, and overall healthcare services.

Persecution and Discrimination: Individuals facing persecution or discrimination based on their ethnicity, religion, sexual orientation, or other factors may seek asylum in the U.S. as a way to escape systemic mistreatment.

Safety and Security: Some individuals may be fleeing violence, insecurity, or persecution in their home countries. They perceive the U.S. as a safer haven and a place where they can escape threats to their well-being.

Political Freedom: Some migrants are motivated by the pursuit of political freedom and democratic values. They may seek to escape political repression or lack of political freedoms in their home countries.

Escape from Armed Conflict: Individuals living in regions affected by armed conflict or war may migrate to the U.S. to escape the dangers and challenges associated with such conflicts.

Desire for a Better Quality of Life: The pursuit of an overall better quality of life, encompassing factors like freedom, social opportunities, and personal fulfillment, is a non-economic motivation for migration.

Escape from Environmental Challenges: Climate change, natural disasters, and environmental challenges can force people to migrate. Seeking refuge from extreme weather conditions, droughts, or other environmental crises is a non-economic motivation for migration. Over time, it can be anticipated that climate factors will become a more dominant force influencing migration worldwide.

Global Migration Patterns: Migration is a global phenomenon, and people often move across borders for various reasons. It is argued that the U.S. should be responsive to the broader dynamics of global migration and contribute to addressing the root causes.

Complex Immigration Policies: Critics of the U.S. immigration system often highlight its complexity and argue that navigating legal channels can be challenging. As a result, some individuals resort to undocumented migration due to perceived difficulties in obtaining legal status.

It's important to note that these motivations are often interconnected, and individuals may have a combination of economic and non-economic reasons for seeking to migrate to the United States. Additionally, immigration policies and global events can influence migration patterns over time.

Employment: One of the most common attractions for immigrants to the United States is the opportunity for employment. Proponents of immigration argue that undocumented immigrants contribute to the U.S. economy through labor and consumption. Illegal or undocumented immigrants are employed in large numbers across a wide range of industries, including food service and food processing and construction, where they account for a sizeable portion of the workforce.

Notwithstanding, the Immigration Reform and Control Act of 1986 made it illegal for employers to knowingly hire or continue to employ undocumented workers. The government set up a kind of "hotline" for employers to verify the status of potential employees. E-Verify is a web-based system that compares information from an employee's Employment Eligibility Verification Form I-9 to government records. However, E-Verify is a voluntary program for most employers. While some states have legislative mandates requiring the use of the system as a condition of business licensing, others are required to participate as a result of a legal ruling. Enforcement is another matter.

Despite that, many undocumented workers have employment rights, including wage and hour rights, and are entitled to workers' compensation benefits in most states. The temptations for an employer to ignore the immigration status of an employee include the desire to retain a valued, long-term employee who lacks proper documentation, the potential cost savings associated with employing undocumented workers, and the avoidance of legal repercussions. Employers may also turn a blind eye to immigration status during the hiring process in order to assemble a workforce that is cheap to employ and minimizes their risk. The dominant force on both sides of the table is money.

Some employers say one thing and do another, and that includes some who are often heard complaining about "illegal immigrants." A Washington Post report revealed that a significant number of non-native workers, including undocumented immigrants, were employed at Trump resorts. A New York Times story reported that there were a number of undocumented immigrants working at Donald Trump's golf club in Bedminster, New Jersey, quoting one employee as saying, "There were many people without papers" working there. The Washington Post also covered a story about undocumented workers being employed at Trump's golf club in Westchester County, New York, where about a dozen employees were fired when it was revealed that they were undocumented immigrants.

Education

There are a myriad of forces driving the issue of immigration. Multi-national companies[1] that are known to recruit international students include Accenture, Adobe Research, Capital One, Cisco Systems, Google, Deloitte, Microsoft, Amazon, and Apple. One international company, ApplyBoard[2], specializes in attracting foreign students. At the same time, foreign students are easy targets for exploitation by employers, paying low wages for long hours or not paying wages that are owed. Foreign students can often accumulate debts that could potentially take a lifetime to repay.

---

1. https://www.forbes.com/sites/forbesbusinesscouncil/2022/10/11/3-strategies-for-businesses-to-recruit-international-students/?sh=68bba7792a32

2. https://www.applyboard.com/

The Forces

Social Media

Social media plays a significant role in illegal immigration in the United States. Smugglers advertise their services, share contact information and communicate with potential victims on Facebook, Twitter (now "X") and Instagram. Migrants use social media, like WhatsApp, to plan routes, learn travel conditions, and potential risks. They also collect information about border security and the experience of other migrants making the journey. Some online groups and forums focus directly on coordinating transportation and raising funds for legal fees. Social media helps to with connections with friends and families in the United States.

Smugglers and human traffickers use social media to spread false information and propaganda about the risks involved. When the U.S. government projects a "get tough" policy, the effect is the opposite of the intent. The message from the traffickers becomes "go now before it gets worse."

Advocates against immigration are not silent on social media, often posting misleading content about immigrants. Fake news is rampant, including claims that immigrants are criminals, a drain on the economy. (The fact is, as a group, illegal immigrants pay more in taxes than some of the larger corporations.) They say immigrants represent a threat to national security. Bots and algorithms amplify the ant-immigrant messages, creating the impression that the positions they advocate are more widespread and popular than they are. They become echo chambers and filter bubbles, making it difficult for people to challenge or to expose different perspectives to the social media audience.

Social media has also been used to promote increased prejudice and discrimination, sometimes leading to violent acts against immigrants or even those who are not immigrants. That only serves to generate fear and anxiety among the immigrants themselves.

The resulting atmosphere has the side effect of creating a chilling effect on free speech or preventing people from speaking out in favor of fair treatment of immigrants. It also makes it more difficult to reform the immigration system to create a more just and humane approach to immigration policy and reform.

News Media

News media, both left and right, play a significant role in shaping public attitudes and perceptions of immigration. While the news media can raise awareness of the challenges of immigration issues and the human stories behind the statistics, they can also amplify misinformation and stereotypes.

The Regulatory Reform Act abolished the decades-old policy of the Fairness Doctrine in broadcasting, signed into law in 1987 by President Ronald Reagan. In the absence of the Fairness Doctrine, broadcast media is no longer obligated to air opposing viewpoints. Negative or inflammatory coverage tends to draw a larger audience and, thus, higher advertising revenues. The result was an uptick in negative stereotypes about immigrants and a decrease in public comprehension of the intricacies of the issue. Public confusion about the issue has made it more difficult for constructive conversations about solutions.

Politics

The pattern of political policy on immigration sways one way and then the other. The result was an uptick in negative stereotypes about immigrants and a decrease in public comprehension of the intricacies of the issue. A 2017 study[1] by the Center for American Progress uncovered a 50% surge in unfavorable news coverage of immigration and a decline in public backing for immigration reform.

A public perception, amplified by some political sources, is that immigrants are responsible for an increase in violence. The numbers do not support the popular rhetoric.

A Cato Institute study in 2017 showed that a 10% increase in immigrant population resulted in a 0.4% DECREASE in the homicide rate. The following year, a National Bureau of Economic Research study reflected a 1% increase in the immigrant population on a county level affected the violent crime rate by only 0.23% with an increase in property crime of 0.19%.

---

1. https://www.americanprogress.org/article/facts-immigration-today -2017-edition/

Another popular meme is that immigrants are responsible for the influx of illegal drugs into the United States. Evidence indicates that illicit fentanyl is primarily brought into the U.S. by American citizens, usually through legal ports of entry. The Drug Enforcement Administration (DEA) has stated that the majority of fentanyl is now coming in through the southern border field offices and ports of entry, with Mexican cartels and transnational criminal organizations being the key players in the smuggling operations. Those trying to bring drugs across the border are most likely to be caught by border agents.

Because there are no simple causes, there can be no simple solutions. To understand the complexity, we may want to add up the numbers.

The Numbers

Dying to get in

Since 1998, over 8,000 undocumented migrants have died trying to cross the border. The years 2020 and 2021 broke records for immigrant fatalities on crossing the border. The Rio Grande River at Eagle Pass on the Texas border is often the site of immigrants drowning trying to cross over from Mexico. Nine died in one day in September 2022. The drowning of a woman and her two children made the news reports in January 2024. They were not the only ones to die there that day. The fire chief of nearby Eagle Pass is quoted as saying they respond to the river to recover at least one body a day, including one three-year old infant found floating in the river. [1]

Not all were as a result of drowning. The "deadliest human smuggling event" in U.S. history was 53 immigrants who were left in the back of a tractor trailer without food or water in the sweltering Texas sun. They were abandoned by human traffickers to die.

---

1. https://youtu.be/UehWCWMGahE?si=InHVLT2zQmrvJHV2

Others fall victim to falling or from thirst or exhaustion in temperatures that can reach 118°F (47.7°C).

Arrests

In 2023 there were 2.4 million apprehensions at the Southern border with Mexico. This number does not reflect successful border crossings. It doesn't even account for all borders. Add in the Canadian border, and the number rises to 2.3 million for that year. That number surpassed the 1.7 million apprehended in2021. Many more slip through the system and are described as the "got-aways".That number can be as high as 1,000 per day, totaling 614,000 in 2022. That number is most likely not accurate. The CBP is the Customs and Border Patrol. Former CBP chief Mark Morgan is quoted as saying the number could be over one million.

The country of Venezuela has been in turmoil for the last several years, which resulted in 58,833 arrests of people coming from that country in September 2023. Further down the scale were 2,099 Russian nationals who were stopped in Augusts of that year.

In 2023, 1.23 million people were issued a "Notice to Appear" (NTA) before the immigration court. The backlog is staggering.

The Cost

The budget for the CBP was $14,643 billion in 2022, with the addition of over $1 billion added by the Biden White House. Of that amount,

$6,159 billion was for operations and hiring. That was a 26% increase from the previous year. In 2023, the figure rose to $16 billion, and the budget proposed for 2024 was $25 billion for CBP and Immigration and Customs Enforcement.

In addition, the state of Texas approved $1.5 billion to fund barriers on the border in response to "record-breaking activity."

The cost to the government is only one part of the cost picture. In some cases, individuals may pay several thousand dollars to human smugglers to facilitate their journey. The cost may cover transportation, forged documents, and assistance in navigating the often dangerous routes.

While the majority of people crossing the U.S.-Canada border are not typically engaging in smuggling, those who do may pay fees that vary, depending on the complexity of the journey. It's important to note that the vast majority crossing the U.S.-Canada border are asylum seekers or individuals seeking to reunite with family members rather than engaging in smuggling.

Canadian authorities uncovered a human trafficking case with a tragic ending. The case[2] involves the tragic death of the Patel family, who froze to death while attempting to cross into the United States from Canada. The family, consisting of Jagdish Patel, his wife Vaishali, and their 11-year-old daughter Vihangi, died of exposure on January 19, 2022, near Emerson, Manitoba. The incident has led to charges of human trafficking, homicide, and conspiracy against individuals accused of involvement in the smuggling operation. One of the accused, Fenil Patel, is living outside

---

2. https://www.cbc.ca/news/canada/patel-family-death-accused-human-smuggler-1.7092020

Toronto and has been identified by Indian police as one of the individuals who helped transport the Patel family.

The Patel family paid the smugglers the equivalent of $100,000 for their journey into the United States.

The People

In 2022, the Migration Policy Institute[3] reported that there are now 10.6 million Mexicans living in the United States, making them the largest percentage of illegal immigrants. Estimates are about half are undocumented. It may be surprising to note the next highest number is from India, at 2.71 million, followed by the Chinese, with 2.38 million, and Filipinos, with 1.98 million. Another 1.42 million are from El Salvador, with 1.11 million from Guatemala and 1.01 million from Korea.

To put the numbers in balance, 76% of immigrants from all countries are here legally.

In 2022, there were 78,433 deportations for overstaying their visas. The highest number of such deportations was 359,000 in 2019. Those who are caught can be banned from reentering the country for from three to ten years. Under "expedited removal", the Biden administration can now deport people without a court hearing unless they are claiming asylum. However, there are some countries where the U.S. does not have a return migration agreement, which was the case for Venezuela for seven years until

---

3. https://www.migrationpolicy.org/

2023. Even so, 72,000 Venezuelans who arrived in this country before July 31st of 2023 were offered Temporary Protected Status.

Language and Education

It's estimated that 35% of the immigrant population speaks no English or only a small amount. It may not be widely known that the Cuban government prohibits teaching English in schools or universities. 32% of the adults in the United States who were born outside the country do not have a high school diploma, compared to 11% of the people who were born here.

The Path to the Border

If you are not familiar with the maps of South and Central America, perhaps you should be. The path from South America[1] to the U.S. border begins in Colombia and continues through Panama, Costa Rica, Nicaragua, Honduras, and El Salvador, Guatemala and Belize, and finally Mexico. The conditions in Central American countries are not attractive. For those wishing to escape the turmoil in Venezuela, for example, the journey begins in neighboring Colombia.

As it was described to me in an interview, the laws in Colombia are "very flexible". Anyone who enters Colombia, legally or not, has no problem staying or working there. However, that country, like its eastern neighbor, is experiencing serious inflation, affecting services, food and housing. In Colombia, small companies there, as in Venezuela, take advantage of the lack of regulation by paying very low wages and evading social security payments.

---

1. https://www.worldatlas.com/geography/latin-american-countries.html

Cuba has a significant presence and influence in Venezuela[2], and Cuban security officials help maintain government control. The two countries have a long history of close ties. Venezuela provides subsidized oil to Cuba in exchange for Cuban doctors, teachers, sports trainers, and military advisors. The relationship benefits Cuba more than Venezuela, which serves to worsen conditions in Venezuela. Overall, however, Venezuela gets the short end of the deal.

To a great extent, Venezuela has historically been its own worst enemy. The weakening of that country's economy stems from a combination of poor policy decisions, economic mismanagement and continued political turmoil. Adding to that was a drastic economic decline, with non-oil GDP declining by almost 19 percent combined with a 65% decline in oil revenue from 1978 to 2001[3].

But things may get better. That economy shows signs of growth and there was an agreement between the government and opposition parties. The government and the political opposition have signed an agreement on electoral guarantees for future elections. That could pave the way for possible U.S. sanctions relief, which in turn may diminish the number of people fleeing repression and economic hardship.

Conditions in Colombia, specifically, the town of Cúcuta on the border with Venezuela, were described to me by someone living there this way:

---

2. https://www.cnn.com/2019/02/02/americas/venezuela-cuba-history-oil/index.html

3. https://www.hks.harvard.edu/publications/venezuela-chavez-anatomy-economic-collapse

With a minimum monthly salary of 1,300,000 pesos (appox. $314.10 USD), the majority of Colombians struggle to cover rent expenses of over 300,000 to 500,000 pesos in the most humble neighborhoods, and in less touristy cities like Cúcuta, costs of services such as energy, water, gas and internet over 300,000 pesos in the lowest strata. It almost adds up to the entire salary and food is still missing, which worries people more because the family [food] basket [cost] goes up. For example, with prices of 35,000 pesos ($8.79 USD) for a kilo of meat, [a family] will only be able to put it on the table once or twice a month at most.

And so, for many who find themselves seeking refuge in Colombia, the journey continues northward.

The jungle between Colombia and Panama has become a highway for hundreds of thousands of migrants from around the world, despite its previous reputation as an almost impenetrable barrier. The journey is extremely treacherous, with migrants facing challenges such as dangerous terrain, exposure to disease, and violence at the hands of criminal groups.

Migrants from South America pass through countries like Panama, Costa Rica, Nicaragua, Honduras, and Guatemala. Each country may pose different challenges and opportunities for migrants, including border controls, transportation, and access to resources.

The Darién Gap

Migrant camps in the Darien Gap along the trail from Colombia through the Panama jungle. (Image: MidJourney)

The Darién Gap[4] has become a key access point for people migrating from South America, and the number of migrants crossing this region could reach record highs, with over 251,000 migrants having made the trek as of July 2023. The route is a treacherous and remote jungle region that serves as a critical point for migrants traveling from South America to North America. It is a 60-mile stretch of mountainous jungle linking Colombia and Panama. Migrants, including those from Venezuela and Haiti, cross this region as part of their journey to the United States, Mexico, or Canada.

The pathway is extremely dangerous due to its geography, exposing migrants to risks such as robbery, rape, human trafficking, wild animals, insects, lack of clean water, and difficult terrain. Many migrants suffer from sickness, severe dehydration, and injuries while hiking through the challenging terrain, and some have tragically lost their lives in the process. There are no accommodations, food sources or cell service along the way. As a result, records show that between 2014 and 2021, more than 250 migrants died or went missing while passing through the Gap.

Despite these dangers, the Gap has become the primary passageway for migrants heading to the United States and other northern destinations, as other routes are riskier or more easily blocked. The increasing movement

---

4. https://www.texastribune.org/2023/06/27/texas-migrants-darien-gap-immigration/

of individuals through the Darién, even after efforts to dissuade or prevent migration, demonstrates the significant challenges in addressing this migration route. The lack of safe pathways and the imposition of movement restrictions have pushed more migrants to cross the Darién Gap, exposing them to abuse and enabling an increase in organized crime in the area.

The Darién has become a pathway of last resort for many migrants, with the lack of safe and legal pathways for migration contributing to the increasing movement of individuals through this treacherous region. Migrants are pushed to cross due to a combination of factors prompting individuals to make this perilous journey. Many of the crises compelling people to leave their countries, such as repression, economic insecurity, and political instability. For example, since January 2022, over 440,000 Venezuelans crossed the Darién Gap fleeing the continuing crisis in their country. Add to that the movement restrictions, often promoted by the United States, which have pushed migrants and asylum seekers to cross the Gap, exposing them to abuse and empowering organized crime in the area. Beyond that, many migrants in South America and the Caribbean face difficulties getting visas to Mexico, making the route through the Darién has become more established, with migrants sharing information about the best ways to cross it.

Migrants crossing the Darién Gap are primarily from countries such as Venezuela, Haiti, and Ecuador. It has become a critical passageway for individuals fleeing political instability, economic insecurity, and other crises in these countries.[5] For example, most arrivals in Panama after crossing through the route have been from Venezuela, Haiti, and Ecuador, with

---

5. https://www.hrw.org/news/2023/10/10/how-treacherous-darien-gap-became-migration-crossroads-americas

over 209,000 migrants crossing from January through August 2023[6], the highest number from any group. The increasing movement of individuals from these countries through the Darién Gap reflects the significant push factors driving migration in the region. The Darién jungle, once considered impenetrable, is now crossed by migrants in as little as 2 ½ days, often with the aid of paid guides. Additionally, the Darién has also seen the movement of people from outside the Western Hemisphere, including individuals from the Middle East, South Asia, and sub-Saharan Africa, who first travel to South America and then use the it to reach the United States or Canada.

The traffic of migrants from South America and the Caribbean through the Gap increased in 2015 when faced with increased difficulties getting visas to Mexico and other Central American countries. The Gap became the alternative. After 2021, three quarters of the migrants arriving at the gap were from Haiti, Cuba, and Brazil, along with the children of Haitian migrants living in South America. In 2022, the balance shifted and the majority crossing the jungle gap were from Venezuela. That increase has been traced to recent visa requirements for Venezuelans enacted by Mexico and several Central American countries.

Panama

Not all migrants passing through Central America are from South America. The country of Panama has registered migrants from at least 60

---

6. https://time.com/6547992/migrants-crossing-darien-gap-2023/

African and Asian countries, including Afghanistan and India. Someone I interviewed who had traveled through the Gap commented on the surprising number of people from Europe, Asia and Africa, who were among those on the trail.

There is more than one pathway or route through the gap, and they come with differing tolls. The fees can range from a few hundred dollars USD and upwards. The Chinese, for example, who are willing to pay fees between $1 and $2,000, are guided to safer and shorter routes, sometimes by sea.

Migrant traffic through Panama is not without impact on that country's infrastructure and economy. Near the border crossings and transit routes there has been an increased demand for goods and services, leading to opportunities for local businesses in that region. However, at the same time, that has lead to competition for jobs, particularly low-skilled jobs. At the same time, migrant traffic creates a strain on local services, to the point where local communities face challenges in meeting the needs of both residents and migrants. Environmental impacts cannot be ignored, either. Deforestation and waste disposal are among the detrimental effects.

Panama's governmental policies and international relations have also been affected as friction has developed with neighboring countries and international organizations. During the COVID-19 pandemic, Panama faced the same public health concerns and costs as other nations, complicated by the migrant influx.

One of the rivers migrants often cross by ferry boat while traveling from Panama to Mexico is the Usumacinta River. The Usumacinta River forms part of the natural border between Mexico and Guatemala. Migrants may use boats or ferries to cross this river as part of their journey through Central America, heading northward. The river forms part of the natural border between Mexico and Guatemala. Migrants may use boats or ferries to cross this river as part of their journey through Central America, heading northward. It's worth noting that migration routes and methods can vary, and the specific river crossings may change based on factors such as local conditions, government policies, and law enforcement activities.

Costa Rica and Nicaragua

The influx of migrants has led to changes in border enforcement and asylum procedures in Costa Rica. Costa Rica has often been a transit country for migrants traveling northward through Central America. Many migrants, particularly from countries in South America and Africa, have passed through Costa Rica on their journey to the United States. The influx of migrants passing through Costa Rica has, at times, strained the country's resources and infrastructure. There have been instances where shelters and services intended for migrants have faced capacity challenges. Some migrants may find temporary shelter in refugee camps or immigration detention centers along the way. These facilities can vary in conditions, and migrants may face legal hurdles as they navigate immigration processes.

Nicaragua's political context can influence the experience of migrants. Political stability or instability can impact the treatment of migrants, and government policies may evolve based on the political climate.

Safety for migrants in both Costa Rica and Nicaragua can be subjective and context-dependent. While these countries have generally been seen as more stable and safer compared to some of their neighbors, migrants can face challenges such as discrimination, exploitation, and vulnerability to criminal activities. Safety can also be influenced by the migrants' legal status and the circumstances under which they are traveling.

Honduras, El Salvador and Guatemala

Those who manage to reach Honduras may be joined by others who begin their journey in that country, for many of the same reasons, including the economic challenges, the prevalence of violence and political instability.

The city of San Pedro Sula in Honduras is a significant starting point for many. As migrants travel through Honduras, El Salvador, and Guatemala, they often encounter a range of conditions and challenges. These Central American countries are part of the migration routes that individuals and families follow on their journey northward, seeking better opportunities or refuge. Conditions can vary based on factors such as political stability, economic development, and social circumstances.

Honduras has faced challenges related to high levels of violence and crime, including gang violence and drug-related crime. Migrants may be at risk of encountering violence during their journey. Corruption within government institutions can create challenges for migrants and may contribute to a lack of effective support systems.

Migrants travel through El Salvador by various means of transportation, including buses or walking. El Salvador has faced issues related to gang violence, particularly involving groups like MS-13 and Barrio 18. Migrants may be at risk of extortion, violence, or recruitment by gangs. Migrants from South America often find themselves joined by native of El Salvador motivated by limited access to education and employment opportunities in that country.

Guatemala is a key transit country on the migration route, involving challenges including checkpoints and border controls. That country grapples with high levels of poverty and economic inequality. Migrants may be motivated to leave in search of improved economic prospects. While not as bad as in some neighboring countries, Guatemala has experienced violence and crime, which can impact the safety of migrants. Criminal organizations and human traffickers may exploit vulnerable migrants at many points along the journey, making their journey perilous, and that danger continues to be present in Mexico.

Traveling through Mexico

Migrants who successfully cross into Mexico continue their journey through the country. This may involve long journeys on foot, by bus, or other means of transportation.

Oaxaca, Mexico: Wood and mud cabin used for holding migrants hostage until they were able to pay a fee to bandits. (Image used with permission of the photographer)

Often, along the route, bandits may demand fees for passage and hold migrants hostage. The hostages can be held in cabañas or "cabins" for days at a time. The bandits receive payment through various means, including cash transfers from the migrants' relatives or diaspora networks. Migrants reach out by phones to their friends or relatives, often in other countries, to arrange payment. The bandits may also use the victim's phones to directly negotiate a ransom.

Once the payment is made, the bandits release the hostages.

The migrants often also face challenges related to law enforcement, some of whom may also be corrupt.

Some migrants seek asylum in Mexico or plan to continue their journey to the United States. That involves navigating the asylum application process and complying with the immigration laws of the respective countries. Migrants who choose to stay in Mexico may work on integration into the local communities. Others may continue their journey, facing additional challenges as they approach the U.S.-Mexico border.

Reaching the U.S. Border

For those who manage to complete the trip to the Southern U.S. border, the journey is not over. Contrary to rumor, the U.S. border is not open. Migrants may be detained in U.S. immigration detention centers while their cases are being processed. The processing time for migrants in U.S. immigration detention centers can vary widely depending on several factors, and there isn't a fixed or typical duration. The length of the process is influenced by the individual's specific immigration case, the complexity of their situation, and the overall efficiency of the immigration system.

Meanwhile, they face inadequate facilities and overcrowding and difficult humanitarian conditions.

The asylum process involves interviews and hearings, but there may be delays and challenges in accessing a fair and efficient system. And the rules can change. Shifts in political administrations may lead to changes in policies between the time they leave their home country to the time when they reach their destination at the southern U.S. border.

Alternate Routes

Irregular migration to the US East Coast occurs through other routes, including the Caribbean and the Bahamas. The Bahamas attracts migrants due to its relatively lenient visa requirements. As a result, the Bahamas has become a significant transit point, attracting migrants from around the world.

Migrants arrive in the Bahamas from China, Cameroon, Iraq and other places in the Caribbean by air and then attempt to reach the U.S. East Coast by boat. The U.S. Coast Guard intercepts a significant number of migrants, but thousands are not intercepted and manage to reach the U.S. shores.

There are other routes that begin with a flight to Guyana on the coast and continue to South and Central America by land.

Not to overlook the northern border. Immigrant traffic through the Canadian border with the United States has increased. Migrants have been seeking asylum at the U.S. Canada border or attempt to cross into the United States. Asylum-seekers arrive legally at airports across the country. New York has become an immigration corridor and a hub for human trafficking. Migrants board flights from Mexico to Toronto or Montreal and contact smugglers to cross the U.S. border. To some, that route is attractive because of the absence of gangs. Mexicans are not required to have a visa to enter Canada. As such, every American airport becomes a border crossing.

Those who can't travel by air must face many barriers along their path to the border.

The Barriers

The Barriers

Structural and Socio-Cultural Barriers: Syrian refugees and asylum seekers in Switzerland face multiple structural and socio-cultural barriers, including language barriers, gatekeeper-related problems, lack of resources, lack of awareness, fear of stigma, and a mismatch between the local health system and perceived needs. Socio-cultural barriers include a dissonance between cultural systems of the country of origin versus the host country, stigma, lack of mental health awareness, and cultural mismatch between refugees' and asylum seekers' problems and needs and the health system in the host country.

Cultural Competence in Service Settings: Refugees and asylum seekers, despite their diverse cultural backgrounds and nationalities, often share common experiences. They may face challenges accessing services that address their individual and cultural needs, requiring cultural competence in service settings to effectively address their unique experiences and challenges.

Impact of Policy Changes: Changes in asylum policies and expedited hearings can impact asylum grant rates and the processing time of asylum cases. Expedited hearings have been successful at shortening the time to process an asylum case for an increasing volume of cases, but they have also impacted asylum grant rates, representation, and the filing of full asylum applications.

Lack of Interpreters: Language barriers can prevent asylum-seekers from effectively communicating their experiences and reporting abuse they have experienced in detention, potentially hindering their ability to present their case effectively. Language barriers can make refugees feel isolated, hopeless, and anti-social, leading to depression. Struggling with speaking and comprehension can make it difficult for refugees to make friends with peers and can unfortunately make them a target of bullying. Asylum seekers who speak rare languages may face challenges in accessing language interpretation services and obtaining interviews in their native tongue, leading to delays in the processing of their asylum cases. Language barriers can hinder access to mental healthcare among refugees and asylum seekers, as they may face difficulties in understanding how the local health system works and in effectively communicating their mental health needs.

Unique and Complex Needs: Refugees and asylum seekers have unique and complex needs related to their experiences of forced displacement and resettlement. These needs may differ from those of other immigrant populations, and they often share common experiences, including trauma, torture, loss or separation of family members, hardships of flight, stigma, discrimination, social isolation, and financial insecurity.

These examples illustrate how social and cultural factors, including unique and complex needs, cultural competence in service settings, and structural and socio-cultural barriers, can complicate asylum cases and influence their processing time and outcomes.

What is the process for legal entry into the United States from a foreign country? How long does it take?

The average processing time for asylum cases in the United States can range from several months to several years, depending on various factors such as the type of application, the backlog of cases, and the specific circumstances of each case.

Affirmative Asylum Process: The average wait times for cases in the asylum backlog averages 1,525 days, according to the American Immigration Council. This means the processing time for asylum cases can extend over several years.

Asylum Backlog: The average processing time for asylum cases in the United States can range from several months to several years, depending on various factors, such as the type of application, the backlog of cases, and the specific circumstances of each case. The backlog of asylum cases pending in U.S. immigration courts has been growing, with wait times averaging 1,621 days, translating into roughly 54 months or nearly four and a half years.

Asylum Work Permit Applications: USCIS data indicates that it's currently taking 5.5 to 12 months to process work permit applications (Form I-765) for individuals with approved asylum status.

Historical Processing Times: Historical processing times for asylum work authorization applications have varied widely, with the average processing time for an asylum work permit (Form I-765[1]) being 3.4 months over the last five years.

Legal Barriers: Certain legal barriers, such as the one-year filing deadline for asylum applications and the potential ineligibility for asylum if the deadline is not met, can affect the timely filing of asylum cases.

---

1. https://www.uscis.gov/sites/default/files/document/forms/i-765.pdf

Complex Process: The asylum process is complex and involves multiple federal agencies. As reported by PBS NewsHour, it can last from a few months to a few years.[2]

Case Complexity: Asylum cases can be exceedingly complex and are influenced by complex life histories and political and social contexts outside of the United States.

Expedited Hearings: The implementation of expedited hearings and the growth of dedicated dockets for asylum cases have led to a significant increase in the number of asylum cases being decided within 3 to 18 months. However, expedited hearings have also impacted asylum grant rates, with a decrease in grant rates for cases closed within 3 to 18 months.

What are the restrictions?

Resource Allocation: The allocation of resources, including the capacity of the CBP Office of Field Operations to process asylum seekers at ports of entry, can influence the processing time of asylum cases.

Political and Social Contexts: Asylum cases are influenced by complex life histories and political and social contexts outside of the United States. The political and social conditions in the asylum seekers' home countries can impact the processing time of asylum applications. For instance, an increase in asylum claims from individuals originating from a particular

---

2. https://www.pbs.org/newshour/politics/how-the-u-s-asylum-proce
ss-works

country due to ongoing conflicts or human rights issues may lead to longer processing times as resources are allocated to address the influx of cases.

Discretionary Nature of Asylum: Asylum is discretionary, and asylum applications may be approved or denied based on an Immigration Judge's individual conclusions about a case. The discretionary nature of asylum decisions can contribute to the complexity of asylum cases and impact the processing time.

What are the answers?

Overcoming language barriers in asylum cases is crucial for ensuring effective communication and equitable access to the asylum process. Here are some ways to overcome language barriers in asylum cases:

Professional Language Interpreters: Utilize professional language interpreters to facilitate effective communication with asylum seekers. This ensures accurate interpretation and helps asylum seekers express their experiences and needs effectively.

Patient Preferences: When selecting an interpreter, consider the preferences of asylum seekers, including their language preferences and other factors that may impact effective communication.

Awareness of Local Language Interpreting Services: Be aware of local arrangements for language interpreting services, including funding, to ensure access to professional interpretation services for asylum seekers.

Avoiding Use of Friends or Relatives as Interpreters: Refrain from using friends or relatives as interpreters, as this may prevent asylum seekers from disclosing sensitive health issues, hindering the provision of safe and effective care.

Access to Rare Language Interpreters: For asylum seekers who speak rare languages, ensure access to interpreters proficient in these languages to facilitate effective communication and understanding during the asylum process.

Cultural Competence: Develop cultural competence in service settings to effectively address the unique experiences and challenges faced by asylum seekers and ensure that their cultural and linguistic needs are met.

Policy Considerations: Consider policy changes that address language access in the asylum system, ensuring that asylum seekers have access to interpretation services that enable effective communication and understanding.

By implementing these strategies, the asylum process can be more accessible and equitable for asylum seekers, ensuring that language barriers do not hinder effective communication and understanding during the asylum process.

How Can Technology Help?

Technology can be used to overcome language barriers in asylum cases in several ways, including:

Language Interpretation Apps: Utilizing language interpretation apps and digital platforms that provide real-time interpretation services can help bridge language gaps between asylum seekers and legal professionals, facilitating effective communication during asylum interviews and legal proceedings

Access to Rare Language Interpretation: Leveraging digital technologies to access rare language interpretation services, especially for asylum seekers who speak less common languages, can help ensure that they can effectively communicate their experiences and needs during the asylum process.

Telehealth and Tele-interpretation: Implementing telehealth and tele-interpretation technologies can facilitate remote interpretation services, enabling asylum seekers to access interpretation support for medical and mental health consultations, and overcoming language barriers in healthcare settings.

Digital Language Learning Tools: Providing access to digital language learning tools and resources can help asylum seekers improve their language proficiency, empowering them to communicate more effectively with legal professionals and navigate the asylum process.

By leveraging technology in these ways, the asylum process can be more accessible and equitable for asylum seekers, ensuring that language barriers do not hinder effective communication and understanding during legal proceedings and healthcare interactions.

Video conferencing can be used to overcome language barriers in asylum cases in the following ways:

Remote Interpretation Services: Video conferencing allows for the provision of remote interpretation services, enabling asylum seekers to communicate with legal professionals and healthcare providers through professional interpreters, even if they are not physically present at the location. This can help bridge language gaps and facilitate effective communication during asylum interviews and legal proceedings.

Access to Rare Language Interpretation: Asylum seekers who speak rare languages may face challenges in accessing language interpretation services through video conferencing, potentially leading to delays in the processing of their asylum cases. Video conferencing can facilitate access to rare language interpretation services, especially for asylum seekers who speak less common languages. This can help ensure that asylum seekers can effectively communicate their experiences and needs during the asylum process, even if in-person interpreters for rare languages are not readily available.

Telehealth and Tele-interpretation: Video conferencing technologies can be utilized for telehealth and tele-interpretation, enabling asylum seekers to access remote interpretation support for medical and mental health consultations. This can help overcome language barriers in healthcare settings, ensuring effective communication and understanding between healthcare providers and asylum seekers. By leveraging video conferencing in these ways, the asylum process can be more accessible and equitable for asylum seekers, ensuring that language barriers do not hinder effective communication and understanding during legal proceedings and healthcare interactions.

However, using video conferencing to overcome language barriers in asylum cases can have potential drawbacks, including:

Technical Challenges: Video conferencing may be susceptible to technical issues, such as poor audio or video quality, which can hinder effective communication and understanding between asylum seekers and legal professionals or healthcare providers.

Lack of Adequate Sound and Picture: The use of videoconferencing in immigration court may lead to difficulties due to the lack of adequate sound and/or picture, impacting the respondent's ability to effectively argue their case to the judge.

Ineffective Presentation of Evidence: In some cases, video conferencing may make it difficult to present evidence and translate testimony, rendering the respondent unable to effectively argue their case to the judge.

Impact on Testimony: Video conferencing may affect the perception of asylum seekers, as their appearance on video may not accurately reflect their circumstances, potentially influencing the judge's perception of their testimony.

Cultural Sensitivity: Video conferencing may not adequately address the cultural and linguistic needs of asylum seekers, potentially impacting their ability to effectively communicate their experiences and needs during the asylum process.

These drawbacks highlight the potential challenges associated with using videoconferencing to overcome language barriers in asylum cases. They emphasize the need for careful consideration of the limitations and potential impact on effective communication and understanding during legal proceedings and healthcare interactions.

The Objections

A YouTube video produced by Scripps News in late 2023[1] includes an interview with a volunteer militia member patrolling the Arizona border that reflects the feeling of many:

> *"Without a border you don't have a country. So, right now, we don't have a country. If you bring enough impoverished people into a nation with wealth, that nation collapses and has to turn into a socialist country" (Spokesperson for Arizona Border Recon)*

On the point about poverty...

Based on current reports, payments to a cartel coyote for one person to be delivered across the Mexican border to the United States can range from $1,500 to $2,500 and more for simple routes from nearby locations in Mexico, to as much as $20,000 for concealed crossings in vehicles or routes

---

1. https://www.youtube.com/watch?v=voVUrtDuJDM

promising compromised border officials[2]. Those fees are not what might be expected from "impoverished people."

Of course, prices will vary depending on the crossing method, final destination, time of year or individual negotiation factors. People suffering from poverty would be hard pressed to pay those prices. In that regard, the stereotype doesn't quite fit.

"Why don't they just stay in Mexico?"

That question is often posed in discussions about undocumented immigrants entering the United States. The fact is, Mexico doesn't exactly roll out the welcome mat to immigrants. Mexico has a number of restrictions on foreign ownership of property and employment. These restrictions are designed to protect the Mexican economy and culture.

Employment: Non-citizens generally need a work visa to legally work in Mexico. The type of visa required depends on the nature of the work and the length of stay. Working without the appropriate visa or work permit is illegal. Foreigners can work in Mexico if they have a valid work permit. Work permits are typically issued to foreigners who have a job offer from a Mexican company. Foreigners can also apply for a work permit if they are self-employed or if they are investing in a Mexican business. These regulations aim to ensure that the majority of the workforce in Mexico consists of Mexican nationals while also providing avenues for foreign nationals to work in the country under certain circumstances.

---

2. Source: ChatGPT3.5

Visa Requirements: Mexico has various types of visas for different purposes, such as tourist visas, temporary resident visas, and permanent resident visas. The type of visa a non-citizen needs depends on factors like the intended length of stay, the purpose of the visit, and whether the individual plans to work or conduct business.

Investment: Non-citizens looking to make significant investments in certain sectors in Mexico may be subject to additional regulations. Foreigners are allowed to invest in Mexico, but there are some restrictions. For example, foreigners are not allowed to invest in certain sectors of the economy, such as oil and gas.

Business ownership: Foreigners can own businesses in Mexico, but they must comply with Mexican law. For example, foreign-owned businesses must hire a certain percentage of Mexican workers.

Property ownership: Foreigners are generally prohibited from owning property within 50 kilometers of the coast or 100 kilometers of the border. This is known as the Restricted Zone. In order to own property in the Restricted Zone, foreigners must obtain a permit from the Mexican government. In the restricted zone, non-citizens can acquire property through a bank trust known as a *"fideicomiso"* or by establishing a Mexican corporation.

These restrictions are designed to protect the Mexican economy and culture. However, they can also make it difficult for migrants from other Latin countries to live and work in Mexico.

To protect the Mexican economy: Mexico is a developing country, and its economy is still vulnerable to foreign competition. The government believes that restrictions on foreign ownership of property and employment are necessary to protect Mexican businesses and workers.

To preserve Mexican culture: Mexico has a rich and unique culture, and the government wants to ensure that it is not diluted by foreign influence. The restrictions on foreign ownership of property and employment are seen as a way to protect Mexican culture.

To prevent foreign domination: Mexico has a history of foreign domination, and the government is wary of allowing foreigners to gain too much control over the country's economy or culture. The restrictions on foreign ownership of property and employment are seen as a way to prevent foreign domination.

Breaking the Myths

T here are several immigration myths that need to be addressed. A YouTube[1] video by Robert Reich spelled out five of them.

Myth #1: The Biden Administration does not want to secure the border.

Fact: The claim that the Biden Administration does not want to secure the U.S. border is not supported by actions and policies that have been implemented since President Biden took office. The Biden-Harris Administration has taken various steps to increase border enforcement and manage immigration more effectively, despite challenges and limitations. The Administration has demonstrated a commitment to securing the border through various measures and budget proposals. President Biden requested funding to secure the border, and Republican legislators blocked additional money for customs and border protection. While there are ongoing debates and criticisms regarding the effectiveness of these measures, the actions taken and the policies implemented contradict the claim that the Administration does not want to secure the border.

---

1. https://www.youtube.com/watch?v=vJwom3uYyV8

Myth #2: Immigration causes the drug crisis as illegal immigrants smuggle drugs through illegal border crossings.

Fact: 90% of illegal drugs seized at the U.S. border arrives through official ports of entry. The quantity of drugs seized is not insignificant. According to the CBP, 25,901 pounds of fentanyl was seized crossing the Southwest border in 2022. However, a CATO Institute study reports show that 86% of those convicted of trafficking fentanyl in 2021 were U.S. citizens.

Myth #3: Undocumented immigrants are terrorists.

Fact: A report from the Council on Foreign Relations states that while the fear of illegal immigrants committing acts of terrorism is not entirely unfounded, there is scant evidence that illegal immigrants have committed acts of terrorism in the United States. The total number of people who have been killed in a terrorist attack in the United States involving someone who illegally crossed the border is zero.[2]

Myth #4: Immigrants steal American jobs.

Fact: While there has been a recent surge in the number of immigrants, legal and undocumented, crossing the U.S. border, evidence shows it has not increased unemployment. The claim that immigrants "steal" American jobs is a complex issue and is not supported by a consensus in the research. Many studies suggest that immigrants, both documented and

---

2. https://www.cfr.org/blog/southern-border-poses-terrorism-risks-ho megrown-threats-still-loom-larger

undocumented, often fill jobs that U.S. citizens do not want or are not willing to do.[3]

Myth #5: Immigrants cause crime.

Fact: Undocumented immigrants seek to remain "under the radar" in order to avoid detection and avoid deportation. Nevertheless, during the recent surge in immigration, the national crime rate continued to decline to the larges decrease on record. In 2022, the CBP arrested and detained 32,097 aliens with criminal records, of which 598 were known gang members, and 178 of those belonged to the MS-13 that originated in the United States. However, A 2020 study showed that undocumented immigrants have substantially lower crime rates as compared with the rest of the population or legal immigrants.

The claim that Venezuela is emptying prisons and sending violent criminals to the U.S. southern border has been made by some U.S. politicians, such as Rep. Troy Nehls,[4] who claimed, "DHS confirms that Venezuela empties prisons and sends violent criminals to our southern border." However, fact-checking organizations have not found evidence to support this claim. The lawmakers' assertion is based on a single article from the politically conservative website Breitbart News.

---

3. https://www.pewresearch.org/short-reads/2020/06/10/a-majority -of-americans-say-immigrants-mostly-fill-jobs-u-s-citizens-do-not-w ant/

4. https://www.statesman.com/story/news/politics/politifact/2022/10 /04/fact-checking-claim-on-venezuela-sending-prisoners-to-the-us -border/69535375007/

While there are criminal elements that cross international borders and individuals with criminal records have been found among migrants, the available information does not substantiate the claim that countries are deliberately sending convicted criminals to cross the U.S. border. Official sources have not confirmed claims to the contrary.

While there are criminal elements that cross international borders and individuals with criminal records have been found among migrants, the available information does not substantiate the claim that countries are deliberately sending convicted criminals to cross the U.S. border. Official sources have not confirmed claims to the contrary.

Mexico operates one of the largest immigration detention systems in the world, with facilities known as "migratory stations" and "provisional detention centers" that are used to hold undocumented migrants until their immigration status can be resolved. Migrants are wary of being captured by police or *la migra*.

More on Mexico later. In the meantime, let's review some of the root causes of migration.

The Root Causes

The root causes that motivate migration from South and Central America are not ours to solve. Powers within the United States have done more than enough to contribute to destabilization in that part of the world. The influence of U.S. politics and business interests on the issues faced by countries from which migrants often flee is a complex and multifaceted topic. There are many ways in which U.S. politics and business practices have played a role.

U.S. military interventions in various regions, such as in Latin America and the Middle East, have sometimes contributed to political instability and conflict, leading to displacement of populations. This involvement has included military interventions, support for regimes accused of human rights abuses, and pursuit of geopolitical interests. These interventions have been driven by a range of factors, including economic interests, security concerns, and ideological considerations, shaping the complex history of U.S. involvement in Latin America and the Middle East.

Historically, the U.S. has supported regimes in different parts of the world for geopolitical reasons, even when those regimes were accused of human rights abuses. This support has sometimes fueled resentment and instability.

The U.S. was involved in a coup that led to the overthrow of the left-wing government of Guatemala in 1954 to protect the interests of the

United Fruit Company. The intervention was orchestrated by the U.S. government and the Central Intelligence Agency (CIA) as part of the broader Cold War strategy aimed at containing the spread of communism in the Western Hemisphere. The events surrounding the coup are often referred to as Operation PBSUCCESS.

In Chile in 1973, a military coup ousted President Salvador Allende with the help of the United States, resulting in the creation of the brutal Pinochet regime[1]. The democratically elected socialist government of Allende was overthrown, and General Augusto Pinochet emerged as the new leader, dismantling Congress and outlawing many leftist political parties. The Pinochet regime was characterized by the systematic suppression of political parties and the persecution of dissidents to an extent unprecedented in the history of Chile. The military dictatorship did not end until 1990.

The invasion of Grenada by the United States and a coalition of six Caribbean countries led to the overthrow of that government in 1983. The excuse was the need to protect American nationals and to push back on communist influences. The invasion was known as Operation Fury.[2] After the military operation, Grenada's economic and political system collapsed, leading to high unemployment and food shortages. The country severed ties with socialist nations and became dependent on U.S. aid for rebuilding its economy.

Before the U.S. invasion in 1983, Grenada's economy was already facing challenges. The country's economic mainstay, the nutmeg crop, had been severely impacted by natural disasters, setting the economy back several

---

1. https://en.wikipedia.org/wiki/Military_dictatorship_of_Chile

2. https://dc.cod.edu/cgi/viewcontent.cgi?article=1131&context=essai

years. The main industries in Grenada were agriculture and some limited industrial production. Political instability and internal strife further contributed to the economic difficulties. The country's rugged, volcanic terrain was conducive to the cultivation of fruits such as mangoes, bananas, tamarinds, breadfruit, and various spices, with nutmeg being a significant export crop. However, farming techniques were relatively basic, and industrialization was limited, with token production of furniture, garments, and processed foods. The economy was heavily reliant on agriculture, particularly the nutmeg crop, which suffered setbacks due to natural disasters, impacting the country's export earnings. Grenada's export earnings were also affected, and the country's industrialization was limited, with low productivity and a lack of significant industrial development.

In 1989, the United States invaded Panama and extradited General Manuel Noriega to the United States for trial. Noriega had risen to power in Panama after reportedly manipulating the presidential election in 1984. Noriega was accused of facilitating drug trafficking, particularly cocaine smuggling, and of using Panama as a hub for illegal activities. These allegations heightened concerns in the U.S. Noriega came to the attention of the U.S. government when Panamanian forces killed a U.S. Marine. President George H.W. Bush ordered the invasion of Panama, citing the need to protect American lives, restore democracy, and secure the Panama Canal. The operation involved a large-scale deployment of U.S. military forces. Overall, the invasion had long-lasting economic repercussions for Grenada, leading to its increased reliance on U.S. aid and the destabilization of its economy.

U.S. corporations have been involved in resource extraction in developing countries, sometimes leading to environmental degradation and exploitation of local communities without adequate compensation. Some U.S. companies have been criticized for exploiting cheap labor in developing countries, contributing to economic disparities and social unrest. Critics argue that these activities can lead to environmental degradation, including deforestation, water pollution, and habitat destruction. There have been cases where local communities in developing countries have faced negative impacts from resource extraction without receiving adequate compensation.

The impact of U.S. trade policies, such as the North American Free Trade Agreement (NAFTA), has been a subject of debate. Such agreements can lead to the influx of cheaper imports from the more developed partner (in this case, the U.S.). Such agreements can disadvantage local industries in partner countries, leading to economic challenges and spurring migration.

U.S. anti-drug policies, particularly in Latin America, have been linked to increased violence and instability. Efforts to combat drug trafficking have sometimes unintentionally fueled conflicts and forced people to migrate. Sometimes, efforts to dismantle drug cartels and disrupt trafficking routes have unintentionally fueled conflicts between rival criminal groups or between those groups and security forces. The power vacuum created by targeting key figures in drug organizations has sometimes led to internal strife and competition for control, exacerbating violence.

The United States has historically been one of the largest contributors to global carbon emissions. Burning coal, oil, and natural gas for energy has released substantial amounts of carbon dioxide into the atmosphere, contributing to the greenhouse gas effect. Climate change, exacerbated by industrial practices and carbon emissions, can lead to environmental challenges in other countries, forcing people to migrate due to changing conditions.

The U.S. is a major arms exporter, and weapons sales to conflict-prone regions often contribute to the perpetuation of violence and displacement.

Some argue that U.S. economic dominance and influence in international financial institutions can perpetuate neocolonial dynamics, shaping economic policies in ways that benefit the U.S. but may not be in the best interest of the affected countries. The guns in the hands of the Mexican cartels were largely purchased in Texas.

In short, if we are searching for the causes of immigration, we need look no further than the mirror. Part of the solution must involve not doing those things in the future.

It's important to note that the relationship between U.S. actions and the challenges faced by other countries is complex, and not all migration can be directly attributed to U.S. policies or business practices. Many factors, including local governance, internal conflicts, and historical conditions, also contribute to the situations that prompt people to migrate. Additionally, U.S. policies and actions can have both positive and negative impacts, depending on the context.

Some argue that the historical ties between the U.S. and certain countries, including Mexico, create a shared responsibility for addressing migration challenges. The obstacles facing solutions to the immigration issue come from a myriad of sources. The underlying obstacle is political division. A lack of consensus among both politicians and the public hinders finding pathways to legalization and resolving the role of immigrants in the economy.

The U.S. economy relies on immigrant labor, both legal and illegal. Of necessity, enforcement requires a delicate balance that does not infringe on basic individual rights, which requires refinement of enforcement strategies and mechanisms. Political factors outside the control of the U.S. government continue to add to the problem. Venezuela's continued political and economic instability and authoritarian rule have sped up the displacement crisis in that country. Violence and unrest in post-civil war Columbia continue to cause some of its people to seek security abroad. Honduras, El Salvador, and Guatemala continue to experience gang violence, poverty, and corruption.

When Javier Milei became president of Argentina in 2023, he promised a series of radical reforms to address inflation, which had soured past 70%, widespread poverty, and a looming debt crisis.

While the discussions have covered a broad range of factors related to immigration, there are still several aspects and nuances that could be explored further or additional factors that may influence migration patterns.

Globalization

Globalization is characterized by the increased flow of goods, services, information, and people across borders.

Globalization's ease of communication makes it easier to plan and execute illegal migration. Routes of entry without authorization are disseminated, contributing to the growth of undocumented migration. Certain industries in developed nations face a demand for low-skilled (cheap) labor.

Here are a few considerations:

- The impact of cultural and social factors on migration, including the role of community networks, cultural ties, and the influence of diaspora[3] communities in destination countries.

- The influence of health crises, such as pandemics, on migration patterns, as seen with the COVID-19 pandemic and its effects on mobility and immigration policies.

- Broader global economic trends and their impact on migration, including the rise of technology, automation, and the gig economy, which can influence job opportunities and workforce dynamics.

- The role of education and skill levels in shaping migration patterns, as individuals may migrate in search of opportunities that align with their educational and professional backgrounds.

- The effectiveness of integration policies in destination countries and how they impact the social and economic inclusion of migrants.

- The gender dimension of migration, considering the different experiences and challenges faced by male and female migrants.

- The prevalence of human trafficking and exploitation in the context of migration, as vulnerable populations may be at risk of abuse during their journey or upon reaching their destination.

---

3. Diaspora refers to a large group of people who share a cultural and regional origin but are living away from their traditional homeland.

- Educational opportunities are a motivation for migration, particularly for individuals seeking access to higher education in destination countries.

- Regional variations in immigration dynamics, recognizing that the factors influencing migration can vary significantly between different regions of the world.

- The patterns and implications of temporary and circular migration, where individuals move between their home country and a destination country for specific periods of time.

- The influence of public perception and media portrayal of immigrants on policies and attitudes toward migration.

- The impact of government corruption and political instability in both origin and destination countries on migration patterns.

- The concept of environmental justice and how environmental degradation, climate change, and resource depletion contribute to migration, especially in vulnerable communities.

- The examination of the long-term socioeconomic impact of immigration on both sending and receiving countries.

- The challenges faced by migrants after reaching their destination include issues related to social integration, discrimination, and access to healthcare and education.

These considerations highlight the complexity and multifaceted nature of migration. Each factor interacts with others, shaping the overall landscape of global migration patterns. Future discussions and research can delve deeper into these specific aspects to gain a more comprehensive understanding of the topic.

All too often, the efforts to solve the problem of migration can be counterproductive.

Counterproductive Measures

Counterproductive actions[1], such as toughened border enforcement, can lead to a mismatch between immigration policy actions and the underlying realities of immigration, ultimately resulting in unintended outcomes. This can affect the labor market and economic productivity, as well as create barriers that push immigrants towards unauthorized means of entry and employment. Delays in the processing of asylum claims and a backlog in the immigration court system may compel some individuals to enter unlawfully while awaiting a resolution of their asylum cases.

The minimum hourly wage in the United States is more than some workers in Mexico can earn in a day. That wage difference just over the border is a significant factor behind the number of Mexican immigrants coming into the United States.

The U.S. government's E-Verify program requires employers with 25 or more employees to verify the legal citizenship of their employees. Small companies or contractors with fewer than 25 employees who are not subject to the requirement compete with lower prices against the larger

---

1. https://comparativemigrationstudies.springeropen.com/articles/10.1186/s40878-020-00181-6

companies who are required to comply. Inconsistent or weak enforcement of penalties for employers who hire undocumented workers can create an environment where some businesses are willing to take the risk of hiring unauthorized labor. Several companies have been cited for violating rules against hiring undocumented workers. Some of the consequences include civil and criminal penalties. For example, Speed Fab Crete, a North Texas construction company, agreed to pay $3 million for its role in employing undocumented workers.

Industries or employers that engage in exploitative labor practices, such as paying low wages or providing poor working conditions, may attract individuals who are willing to accept such conditions, including undocumented workers. The Miami Herald reported that restaurants, hotels, construction, and other industries in South Florida are experiencing a severe labor shortage because of the crackdown on undocumented immigrants by Governor DeSantis.

In 2005, Walmart Stores Inc., the nation's largest retailer, settled a federal investigation that found hundreds of illegal immigrants[2] had been hired to clean its stores by paying $11 million. Federal investigators said they had decided not to bring criminal charges against the company when it promised to take strong action to prevent future employment of illegal immigrants. During the investigation, Federal officials arrested[3] about 250 illegal immigrants working on cleaning crews at 61 stores in 21 states.

---

2. https://www.nytimes.com/2005/03/19/business/walmart-to-pay-u s-11-million-in-lawsuit-on-illegal-workers.html

3. https://money.cnn.com/2003/10/23/news/companies/walmart_wo rker_arrests/

In a federal RICO class action suit,[4] employees claimed Wal-Mart hired them knowing they were undocumented, failed to pay for overtime, and paid with cash or personal checks to avoid detection. Testimony in that case claimed that Walmart management realized the company could substantially increase profits by relying on undocumented migrants to clean thousands of stores.

Research published in Comparative Migration Studies[5] indicated that certain immigration policies that are not grounded in a real understanding of the causes or consequences of migration can backfire and speed up the rate of undocumented population growth. This can create a mismatch[6] between immigration policy actions and the underlying realities of immigration, ultimately leading to unintended outcomes.

Measures taken against the availability of birth control and abortion could result in higher birth rates among undocumented migrants living in places like Texas. Those children become U.S. citizens at birth, regardless of the legal status of their parents.

Opposition to immigration often focuses on perceived adverse effects, such as economic costs and negative environmental impact. However, these actions can lead to unintended outcomes, including the reduction of

---

4. https://www.courthousenews.com/class-of-undocumented-workers -sues-wal-mart/

5. https://comparativemigrationstudies.springeropen.com/articles/10. 1186/s40878-020-00181-6

6. https://www.ncbi.nlm.nih.gov/pmc/articles/PMC8547794/

the likelihood of return migration, which can have implications for social welfare systems and community dynamics.[7]

Questions arise as to whether Republicans are sincere about addressing the border problem. In January of 2024, the Huffington Post reported[8] that Donald Trump reached out to some Senate Republicans, telling them he wants them to reject any border deal "...because he doesn't want Biden to have a victory."

Lengthy processing times, bureaucratic hurdles, and inefficiencies in the legal immigration system may push individuals towards illegal methods because of the perceived difficulty of obtaining legal status. Policies that restrict legal immigrants' access to social services may create an environment where undocumented individuals believe they have limited options for support and turn to illegal means for survival.

Many countries face similar problems with unregulated immigration. What solutions have they tried? Do any of them work?

---

7. https://www.cato.org/cato-journal/fall-2017/counterproductive-consequences-border-enforcement#

8. https://www.yahoo.com/news/trump-privately-pressuring-gop-senators-003824529.html

Who Gets It Right?

Which countries have the best immigration policies? Canada is often praised for its point-based system, prioritizing skilled immigrants. Australia and New Zealand also have what appear to be successful immigration systems. Germany, Sweden, and Singapore seem to have fewer immigration problems than most other countries. Singapore, Australia and New Zealand have the advantage of being islands. Of these, there is no common geographic pattern.

Canada

Canada shares the longest undefended border in the world with the United States. The border stretches over 8,891 kilometers (5,525 miles) and
spans from the Atlantic Ocean in the east to the Pacific Ocean in the west. It separates the continental United States and Canada and includes land and maritime boundaries. There are at least 120 border crossing points spanning 5,525 miles. That number includes international airports, seaports and smaller road crossings and major land crossings at the Windsor-Detroit tunnel and the Ambassador Bridge, with the Peace Arch

crossing into Blain, Washington, the Champlain-Saint Bernard de Lacolle, and Niagara Falls crossing into New York. There are no walls.

Canada's system is based on factors such as age, education, language proficiency, work experience, and adaptability. That country celebrates diversity, which has enhanced social harmony. As a result, Toronto's foreign-born population currently amounts to 50%. That level is higher than in major cities in the United States, including Los Angeles, San Francisco, and New York.

Canada invites students, and that has created its own problem. Colleges and schools of all sizes actively promote overseas students. Recruiters in India use false promises to lure students to Canada.

The resulting influx of students has created a severe housing shortage in many provinces, severely raising the costs of housing. Foreign students find themselves sharing housing with a dozen or more other students, often sharing the same bed on a schedule. The cost of living in Canada has been soaring to the extent that housing in Toronto is more expensive than in San Francisco, which has a higher average income.

Post-secondary schools in Canada, both public and private, can charge international students as much as 500% of the fee they can charge domestic students for the same classes. As a result, some have begun aggressive marketing campaigns to lure new foreign students. Canada is reconsidering its liberal student immigration policy and placed a two-year cap on new international student permits. That action is expected to result in a 35% reduction in approved study visas for the year 2024.

Australia

There are no walls around Australia, so what makes their immigration policy better? For one, Australia deters maritime arrivals by turning back boats carrying asylum seekers trying to reach their shores. However, the policy, while deemed effective, has received criticism for possible violations of international law and human rights.

Like Canada, Australia's immigration rules are based on a point-based system designed to attract skilled migrants. That system, too, has received criticism for its strict criteria, which could exclude individuals who could represent a valuable contribution to the country's growth but who fall short of the requirements. Even highly skilled migrants may be excluded if their foreign qualifications are not recognized by Australian standards.

The country's Temporary Protection Visas allow refugees to enter the country but with no clear pathway to permanent settlement.

Housing affordability has been a concern in major cities like Auckland. Immigration-driven population growth can contribute to increased demand for housing, potentially leading to higher prices.

Another drawback is the implication immigrants may have for Australia's indigenous communities. Resulting urbanization can divert attention and resources away from addressing the needs of Australia's indigenous people.

New Zealand

New Zealand's immigration policy, like any other, has both positive aspects and challenges.

Like Australia and Canada, New Zealand uses a point-based system for immigrants and those seeking asylum. The system, aimed at attracting people who can contribute to the country's economy, is based on factors including age, education, work experience, and language proficiency.

To its credit, New Zealand has a refugee resettlement program aimed at providing refuge for those fleeing conflict and persecution, aiding international efforts to support displaced populations.

On the negative side are the challenges and drawbacks of the policy. The impact of immigration tends to be concentrated in urban centers, impacting local infrastructure, housing, and job opportunities. Like Canada, the availability of affordable housing is a concern as resulting population growth results in increased demand and higher prices.

At the same time, not unlike the situation in the United States, the influx of increasing numbers of migrants and refugees has resulted in application backlogs and increased processing time.

Singapore

Immigration issues in Singapore are on a much smaller scale than in Canada, Australia, and New Zealand. Singapore is both a city-state and an island country. It is located in Southeast Asia, at the southern tip of the Malay Peninsula. The main island of Singapore is connected to the Malay Peninsula by a causeway to the north and a bridge to the west. The country consists of the main island, Pulau Ujong, and numerous smaller islands.

What Singapore may be getting right is that it uses a largely merit-based system, similar to but distinct from the point-based systems of other countries. The island nation-state actively seeks to attract global talent, including professionals and entrepreneurs, aimed at enhancing the country's competitiveness and innovation. The result is a diverse and multicultural workplace, benefiting from a wider variety of skills, perspectives, and experience. Singapore also enforces strict immigration laws and regulations, which is made easier by the fact that functions on a smaller scale.

On the negative side are the familiar impacts on job competition for local residents, increased strain on infrastructure, and demands on housing, transportation, and public services.

Singapore has the limitation of a limited land area with a high population density, resulting in congestion and limited public spaces. The country also relies heavily on foreign labor for various sectors, and some industries are overly reliant on foreign workers.

Germany and Sweden

Both Germany and Sweden use point-based immigration systems to attract skilled workers, considering factors such as education, language proficiency, and work experience. Both Germany and Sweden have demonstrated a commitment to humanitarian efforts by providing refuge and participating in international efforts to address the world refugee crises.

Germany has a Blue Card system that attracts highly skilled workers outside the European Union by providing streamlined processing for work and residential permits. It also provides language courses, vocational training, and employment support.

Sweden is known for its humanitarian approach, providing refuge to those fleeing conflict and persecution. Sweden, like Germany, invests in integration programs, including language training and cultural orientation, to support newcomers in adapting to their new environment.

Despite policies targeting skilled migration, Germany still relies on low-skilled labor in certain industries, raising questions about long-term economic sustainability. That country has had a public backlash against immigration, with concerns about economic impacts, cultural clashes, and strains on public services. There is also the common problem of processing delays and system bottlenecks. Added to that, a large number of arrivals, especially during the 2015 refugee crisis, raised concerns about security and the ability to effectively screen and vet individuals entering the country.

Like many countries, Sweden has experienced challenges related to housing affordability, with increased demand contributing to rising property prices. Sweden has also faced integration challenges, including issues related to high unemployment rates among certain immigrant groups and difficulties in social cohesion.

While we can learn from the varied approaches of immigration programs of other nations, it is clear that no country has yet found the magic formula. We can take some lessons from our neighbor, Mexico.

What Does Mexico Do?

Mexico has not experienced the same scale of problems from undocumented immigration to the level faced by the United States for several reasons:

- Mexico has a long history of emigration, with many Mexicans historically moving to the United States for economic opportunities. This emigration has helped to ease domestic economic pressures and unemployment.

- While still 14th in the world economy, Mexico has experienced economic growth and development in recent decades, leading to improved job opportunities and living conditions. This has reduced the push factors for Mexicans to migrate in search of better economic prospects.

- With declining birth rates and a younger population, Mexico's demographic landscape has shifted. This demographic transition has contributed to a more stable labor market within Mexico.

- Stricter immigration policies and increased border enforcement by the United States have made it more difficult for undocumented immigrants to enter and remain in the country. This has deterred some potential Mexican migrants.

- Mexico has also invested in strengthening its own border security, collaborating with the United States to address issues related to human trafficking, drug smuggling, and illegal immigration.

- The Mexican economy has diversified and grown, providing a wider range of employment opportunities within the country. This economic diversification has reduced the reliance on migration as a survival strategy.

- Bilateral agreements between Mexico and the United States have focused on addressing shared challenges related to migration. Agreements like the U.S.-Mexico-Canada Agreement (USMCA) include provisions for labor protections and economic cooperation.

- The proximity of Mexico to the United States has fostered strong social and cultural ties. Many Mexican migrants to the U.S. maintain connections with their home country, contributing to a sense of transnational identity.

- Efforts within Mexico to improve education and social services contribute to greater opportunities for its citizens, reducing the push factors for migration.

- Shifts in the U.S. labor market, including changes in demand for specific types of labor, have influenced patterns of migration. Economic factors, such as job availability, impact the attractiveness of the U.S. as a destination for Mexican migrants.

While Mexico has not faced the same level of problems associated with undocumented immigration as the United States, it's important to note that migration dynamics are complex and influenced by a combination of factors. Economic, social, and political changes in both countries contribute to the patterns of migration observed over time. Mexico places restrictions on foreign ownership of property and employment.

- Non-citizens in Mexico generally need a work visa to legally work. The type of visa required depends on the nature of the work and the length of stay. Working without the appropriate visa or work permit carries strong penalties.

- Mexico has restrictions on non-citizens owning property. In order to own property in the Restricted Zone, foreigners must obtain a permit from the Mexican government. Foreigners are generally prohibited from owning property within 50 kilometers of the coast or 100 kilometers of the border. This is known as the Restricted Zone. In the restricted zone, non-citizens can acquire property through a bank trust known as a *fideicomiso* " or by establishing a Mexican corporation.

- Mexico has various types of visas for different purposes, such as tourist visas, temporary resident visas, and permanent resident visas. The type of visa a non-citizen needs depends on factors like the intended length of stay, the purpose of the visit, and whether the individual plans to work or conduct business.

- Foreigners can own businesses in Mexico, but they must comply with Mexican law. For example, foreign-owned businesses must hire a certain percentage of Mexican workers.

- Foreigners are allowed to invest in Mexico, but there are some restrictions. For example, foreigners are not allowed to invest in certain sectors of the economy, such as oil and gas. Non-citizens looking to make significant investments in certain sectors may be subject to additional regulations.

The restrictions are designed to protect the Mexican economy and culture. However, they can also make it difficult for foreigners to live and work in Mexico.

Here are some of the reasons why Mexico has restrictions on foreign ownership of property and employment:

- Mexico is a developing country, and its economy is still vulnerable to foreign competition. The government believes that restrictions on foreign ownership of property and employment are necessary to protect Mexican businesses and workers.

- Mexico has a rich and unique culture, and the government wants to ensure that it is not diluted by foreign influence. The restrictions on foreign ownership of property and employment are designed to protect Mexican culture.

- Mexico has a history of foreign domination, and the government is wary of allowing foreigners to gain too much control over the country's economy or culture. The restrictions on foreign ownership of property and employment are seen as a way to prevent foreign domination.

The Mexican government is committed to reviewing its restrictions on foreign ownership of property and employment. However, it is unclear when or if any changes will be made.

Within Mexico, there are specific regulations and restrictions for employment for non-citizens. According to the Mexican Federal Labor Law, an employer in Mexico is required to employ at least 90% of Mexican workers. For certain categories of workers, such as technicians and professionals, the workers should be Mexicans unless there are none in that particular specialty, in which case the employer may employ foreign workers temporarily, in a ratio not to exceed 10% of those employed in that specialty.

Additionally, foreign nationals must obtain a valid work visa to work legally in Mexico in exchange for remuneration. There are different types of visas, such as temporary visitor visas and temporary resident visas, which allow foreign nationals to work in Mexico under specific conditions.

These regulations aim to ensure that the majority of Mexico's workforce comprises Mexican nationals while also providing avenues for foreign nationals to work in the country under certain circumstances.

The Mexican government has implemented various measures to manage the large influx of migrants seeking entry into the United States. These measures include increased enforcement in Mexico, joint anti-smuggling operations, and the rapid expansion of the Migrant Protection Protocols (MPP), also known as Remain in Mexico.

The MPP program was intended to send asylum seekers to Mexico while they await their U.S. asylum hearing, thereby reducing irregular flows of migrants to the U.S.-Mexico border. Mexico has increased migrant apprehensions and restricted access to humanitarian visas, particularly for those from Central America. The Mexican government has also been working with the United States to address the root causes of migration, interdict migrants, combat alien smuggling and human trafficking, and encourage burden sharing among countries for sheltering vulnerable migrants. Mexico also has a strong national legal and institutional framework to protect asylum seekers and refugees, promoting their integration into national systems with access to employment, public health services, and education at all levels.

These efforts reflect Mexico's collaboration with the United States and its commitment to managing migration flows while upholding humanitarian principles. The United States and Mexico have agreed on several enforcement measures to manage the migration crisis.

These measures include:

- **Increased Enforcement in Mexico:** Both countries agreed to increase enforcement in Mexico to reduce irregular migration flows.

- **Joint Anti-smuggling Operations:** The U.S. and Mexican governments have conducted joint anti-smuggling operations to combat human trafficking and illegal migration.

- **Migrant Protection Protocols (MPP):** The MPP, also known as Remain in Mexico, has been rapidly expanded. This program sends asylum seekers to Mexico while they await their U.S. asylum hearing, thereby reducing irregular flows of migrants to the U.S.-Mexico border.

- **Acceptance of Migrants:** Mexico has agreed to accept migrants from certain countries, such as Venezuela, Haiti, Cuba,

Nicaragua, Honduras, Guatemala, and El Salvador, who are turned away at the U.S. border. At the same time, Mexico operates one of the largest immigration detention systems in the world, with facilities known as "migratory stations" and "provisional detention centers" that are used to hold undocumented migrants until their immigration status is resolved. Agents known as *la migra* patrol the trains that migrants often use for travel through the country.

These measures aim to deter illegal border crossings, address the root causes of migration, interdict migrants, and combat alien smuggling and human trafficking. Additionally, Mexico has a strong legal and institutional framework to protect asylum seekers and refugees, promoting their integration into national systems with access to employment, public health services, and education at all levels. These efforts reflect the collaboration between the United States and Mexico in managing migration flows while upholding humanitarian principles.

How have the enforcement measures affected the number of migrants crossing the border? The enforcement measures agreed upon by the United States and Mexico have had varying effects on the number of migrants crossing the border. In fiscal year 2022, Border Patrol encountered 2.2 million people illegally crossing the border, and the numbers have decreased to about 1.6 million, although it is still considered high. Additionally, more migrants than ever before who are reaching the United States without prior authorization to enter are now arriving at ports of entry as a result of the parole programs and use of the CBP One app.[1]

---

1. https://www.cbp.gov/about/mobile-apps-directory/cbpone

Mexico's enforcement measures have led to fluctuations in the number of migrants crossing the border, demonstrating the complex and evolving nature of migration management efforts between the two countries.

The changing trends pose new, complex challenges for all aspects of border enforcement operations and processing capacity, demonstrating that the current system is not equipped nor flexible enough. Mexico detained over 444,000 migrants in 2022, 44% more than in the previous year, showing a significant impact on the number of migrants. The U.S. and Mexican governments have agreed on new immigration policies meant to deter illegal border crossings while also opening up other pathways following the end of pandemic restrictions.

So, what are the solutions?

Possible Solutions

While there are general trends associated with each party, individual administrations within both the Republican and Democratic parties have shaped immigration policies based on their unique circumstances, priorities, and the prevailing political climate at the time. The issue of immigration is complex and multifaceted, and approaches to it can evolve over time within each party.

The immigration policies of Republican and Democratic administrations in the United States have varied over the years, and the approaches to the immigration issue have often reflected the priorities, values, and political climates of each party. Here's a general overview of how Republican and Democratic administrations have approached immigration:

Republican administrations have favored policies focused on border security, law enforcement, and a strict approach to immigration control. Administrations, including those of Presidents Ronald Reagan, George H. W. Bush, and George W. Bush, have often emphasized enforcement measures, such as increased border patrols and stricter immigration enforcement. Some Republican leaders have advocated for comprehensive immigration reform, including pathways to legal status for certain undocumented individuals. However, these efforts have faced challenges within the party. From 2017 to 2021, the Trump administration took a more hardline stance on immigration. Policies such as the "Zero Tolerance", family separations, and attempts to limit legal immigration garnered significant attention and controversy.

Democratic administrations have historically advocated for more comprehensive and humanitarian approaches to immigration, including pathways to citizenship for certain undocumented individuals. Democratic leaders, including Presidents Bill Clinton and Barack Obama, have called for comprehensive immigration reform that addresses border security, provides pathways to legal status, and includes humanitarian considerations. The Obama administration implemented the Deferred Action for Childhood Arrivals (DACA) program in 2012, which provided temporary relief from deportation and work authorization for eligible undocumented individuals brought to the U.S. as children. Starting in 2021, the Biden administration signaled a shift in enforcement priorities, focusing on national security threats and individuals with criminal records while prioritizing a more humane approach to immigration. Some Democratic administrations have emphasized addressing the root causes of migration, including economic inequality and violence in the countries of origin, as part of a more comprehensive strategy.

Despite occasional bipartisan efforts, immigration reform has faced challenges in achieving consensus due to political polarization and differences in priorities between parties. Public opinion on immigration varies, and shifts in public sentiment can influence political approaches. Both parties may adapt their positions based on changing public attitudes.

Immigration policies implemented by both Republican and Democratic administrations have faced legal challenges, adding complexity to the policymaking process.

Build the Wall?

The answer is simple, right? Just close the borders! "Complete the wall", along all 1,954 miles of the southern border, over mountains and through rivers. Place thousands of armed guards along the border and at all the border gaps between the United States and Mexico and try to stop entry by the use of ladders and crow-bars or wire cutters. Easy!

As of October 2020, the U.S. Customs and Border Protection reported that there were 669 miles of "primary barrier" along the southern border. How many miles of new primary border wall were built during the Trump presidency?

When Donald Trump said the figure is "over 500 miles," the former president is referring to the total of all wall construction during his presidency, which was actually 458. The cost of the wall repair and construction is estimated to be around \$11 billion[1], which translates to nearly \$20 million per mile.[2] According to a review of federal spending data, the cost of the border wall project increased by billions of dollars due to modifications to contracts, with supplemental agreements and change orders alone adding at least \$2.9 billion to the cost. However, the White House under the Biden administration reported that some segments of the wall cost American taxpayers up to \$46 million per mile.

---

1. https://www.npr.org/2020/01/19/797319968/-11-billion-and-cou nting-trumps-border-wall-would-be-the-world-s-most-costly

2. https://www.texastribune.org/2020/10/27/border-wall-texas-cost-r ising-trump/

However, the word "built" should read "completed." According to a federal report, only 52 miles of new wall construction were completed.

The cost of Trump wall construction was about five times more expensive than the border fencing built during the Bush and Obama administrations.[3] The Trump administration initially proposed adding 1,000 miles of wall but later revised that figure down to 450 miles. The Department of Homeland Security's internal estimate in early 2017 was that the proposed border wall would cost $21.6 billion and take 3.5 years to build. However, that effort would require diverting critical resources away from military training facilities and schools, with some wall segments costing American taxpayers up to $46 million per mile.[4]

That cost does not include the expense of ongoing maintenance due to erosion and deterioration (rust) and other factors. The environmental cost[5] was another matter.

---

3. https://www.texastribune.org/2020/10/27/border-wall-texas-cost-rising-trump/

4. https://www.whitehouse.gov/omb/briefing-room/2021/06/11/fact-sheet-department-of-defense-and-department-of-homeland-security-plans-for-border-wall-funds/

5. https://www.wola.org/analysis/400-miles-of-harm-nothing-to-celebrate-about-border-wall-construction/

6. https://www.cnn.com/2022/11/15/politics/fact-check-trump-announcement-speech-2024/index.html

When Trump left office, there were 280[6] miles where wall construction had been planned but not executed. That leaves 1,285 miles left to build just on the southern border.

The whole conversation ignores the Canadian border with the lower 48 states (5,525 miles). Closing the border with Mexico would still not solve the problem; it would only slow it down or divert traffic to other routes or means. Traffic on that border has increased due in part to efforts to close it.

Take in consideration the fact that large number of "illegal immigrants" simply fly in as tourists, overstay their visas and melt into the general population. Still more arrive by sea, either by boat as was the case during the "Cuban Crisis," or on cruise ships as crew members. Even more arrive legally on temporary work visas and later disappear into the workforce.

Or perhaps we should build detention centers large enough to hold millions of immigrants and asylum seekers and then provide the money to support housing and feeding them for as long as it takes to work through the processing backlog, which could be decades.

Keep in mind that the proposal for immigrants and asylum-seekers to remain in Mexico presents the same impossible problems for Mexico.

It's possible some who are heard complaining the loudest may be secretly benefitting from the low labor cost that immigrants provide themselves.

Discussions and debates center on finding a balanced approach that addresses security concerns while upholding humanitarian values and addressing the root causes of migration. But viable solutions to the complex

---

6. https://www.cnn.com/2022/11/15/politics/fact-check-trump-announcement-speech-2024/index.html

issue will not emerge until the public becomes informed and engages in constructive, informed conversations with those who are most affected.

Closing Borders

Closing borders contributes to the increase in unauthorized migration as migrants seek alternative, often riskier methods. This impacts the safety of migrants and poses challenges to border security. Strict border enforcement and immigration policies can result in labor shortages, particularly in agriculture. Closing borders can also disrupt traditional labor patterns and increase illegal traffic.

Newton's third law of motion states that "for every action, there is an equal and opposite reaction." Close the southern border and migrants will cross at the northern border.[7]

The bottom line is that there are no easy answers. That being said, there are some directions in which solutions might be found.

The general public and those who represent us in government need to become better informed of the pressures and conditions that have brought us to where we are today. In short, a reality check. As citizens, we can't look toward the future until we understand the past, including the political factors involved, both negative and positive, both inside and outside of the United States. The United States is grappling with a complex and

---

7. https://www.nbcnews.com/news/latino/more-asylum-requests-illeg al-crossings-canada-northern-border-rcna126329

multifaceted challenge shaped by historical and economic factors, by racial and philosophical differences, and by perceptions and misconceptions.

The inconsistency of partisan politics has only served to stir the pot without providing any lasting answers to the complex issues facing our borders. For the most part, the picture has been that of a tug-of-war rather than any hint of compromise. Politicians are most often motivated by public perception. Social media and news media motivated by clicks, ratings, and advertising revenue has influenced that public perception to a large part. It is no wonder there has been little progress toward solving the problem, and whatever progress that may have been accomplished is quickly erased after the following election. Opinions are meaningless when they are not based on informed insight.

Efforts by the United States to discourage immigration from Central and South America have faced challenges and criticisms, have been deemed ineffective or have failed to achieve their intended outcomes.

There are reasons these efforts may not have been as successful as intended:

- Many individuals from Central and South America are driven to migrate because of economic factors: poverty, lack of job opportunities, and limited access to education. While the U.S. has added border security measures, these economic factors often outweigh any deterrents for people to seek better economic prospects in the U.S.

- High levels of violence, organized crime, and insecurity in some Central American countries, like Honduras, El Salvador, and Guatemala, contribute significantly to migration. U.S. efforts to discourage migration may not address the fundamental issue of insecurity, making it difficult to dissuade individuals from fleeing dangerous conditions. The United States cut off foreign aid to El Salvador, Guatemala, and Honduras between 2017 and 2020. The Trump administration halted humanitarian funding to these countries in an effort put pressure on their governments to take action to reduce migration to the U.S. It did nothing to solve the problem.

- Stringent immigration policies and limited legal avenues for migration may cause individuals to resort to irregular and often dangerous methods to enter the U.S. When legal pathways are restricted, people are compelled to take the informal and riskier routes.

- The desire for family reunification is a powerful migration motivator. U.S. policies that prioritize family reunification may inadvertently encourage individuals to attempt to join family members already in the U.S. despite the deterrent measures.

- U.S. efforts to discourage migration may not effectively address the needs of asylum seekers and individuals fleeing persecution or violence. Humanitarian concerns often override deterrence measures, especially for those seeking protection.

- U.S. border enforcement measures may lead to shifts in migration routes rather than an overall decrease in migration. For example, migrants might choose alternative pathways or countries to reach the U.S., adjusting their routes in response to changing enforcement measures.

- Addressing the root causes of migration, such as economic inequality, corruption, and violence, requires comprehensive and sustained efforts. Simply focusing on deterrence measures may not effectively address the underlying issues that drive people to migrate.

- Political and legal challenges, including legal battles over immigration policies, can impact the implementation and effectiveness of deterrence measures. Court decisions and policy changes may affect the continuity and success of these efforts.

- The messaging and public perception surrounding U.S. immigration policies can influence their effectiveness. Negative public perception or inconsistent messaging may undermine the intended deterrent effect.

- Building effective collaborations with sending countries is crucial. Addressing the root causes of migration requires diplomatic and cooperative approaches, and strained relationships with these countries can hinder the success of U.S. initiatives.

- Shifting geopolitical and regional dynamics, as well as economic changes can influence migration patterns. Factors beyond the U.S.'s control may impact the effectiveness of its efforts.

It's important to note that opinions on the effectiveness of U.S. immigration policies vary, and the issue is complex with no simple solutions. Critics may argue that a more holistic and humanitarian approach, addressing the root causes of migration, may yield more lasting results.

Policy Changes

The inconsistency of partisan politics only serves to stir the pot while providing no lasting answers to the complex issues facing our borders. Republican administrations have emphasized border security and strict enforcement measures, while Democratic administrations have leaned towards comprehensive reform, emphasizing humanitarian considerations and pathways to legal status. Despite these varying approaches, the issue remains deeply polarized, hindered by political gridlock, evolving public opinion, and legal challenges.

For the most part, the picture has been that of a tug-of-war rather than any hint of compromise. Public perception often motivates politicians. Social and news media, motivated by clicks, ratings, and advertising revenue, heavily influence that public perception. It is no wonder there has been little progress toward solving the problem, and whatever progress may have been accomplished is quickly erased following the next election.

Addressing immigration challenges requires a multifaceted approach that considers both enforcement measures and broader policy changes. While effective enforcement of employment rules can be part of the solution, it's important to approach immigration issues in a comprehensive approach. Opinions are meaningless when they are not based on informed insight.

Here are some policy changes and considerations that could contribute to a more holistic approach:

- Enforce existing rules about hiring undocumented workers. Make

E-Verify mandatory. **Fewer jobs means lower incentives for undocumented workers.**

- Adopt a rule like Mexico's where 90% of a company's employees must be citizens, and then allocate adequate funds for enforcement.

- Pass budgeting for the Border Patrol and immigration processing resources that more closely approximate the scope of the problems they are tasked with addressing.

- Pursue comprehensive immigration reform that addresses various aspects of the immigration system, including pathways to legal status for undocumented individuals, improvements to legal immigration processes, and mechanisms for addressing the root causes of migration.

- Invest in technology and infrastructure for border security, ensuring effective monitoring and control of entry points. However, recognize that border security measures alone are insufficient and should be complemented by other policies.

- Collaborate with Central and South American countries to address the root causes of migration, including economic inequality, violence, and corruption. Support development programs that promote stability and economic opportunities in the region.

- Prioritize humanitarian considerations, especially for asylum seekers and individuals fleeing persecution. Develop policies that uphold international humanitarian standards and ensure fair and efficient processing of asylum claims.

- Expand legal avenues for migration to provide individuals with legitimate pathways to enter the U.S. This could include reforms to family reunification, employment-based immigration, and the diversity visa program.

- Strengthen enforcement of employment rules to discourage the hiring of undocumented workers. This strategy may include effective implementation of the I-9 requirement and increased penalties for non-compliance.

- Explore and expand guest worker programs to meet the demand for labor in sectors such as agriculture. Well-regulated guest worker programs can provide legal avenues for temporary employment while minimizing the risks associated with undocumented labor.

- Implement public education campaigns to provide accurate information about immigration policies, legal pathways, and the consequences of illegal entry. Clear messaging can help manage public perception and discourage unauthorized migration.

- Engage with local communities, NGOs, and advocacy groups to better understand the needs and concerns of both immigrant populations and the broader community. Building trust and collaboration can enhance the effectiveness of policies.

- Create pathways to legalization for certain undocumented populations, such as those who have been long-term residents, contributing members of society, or individuals brought to the U.S. as children (Dreamers).

- Review and adapt asylum policies to address evolving global and regional challenges. Consider policies that provide protection to those facing humanitarian crises and persecution.

- Work collaboratively with international organizations, neighboring countries, and sending nations to develop coordinated approaches to migration challenges. Diplomacy and collaboration are essential for addressing global migration issues.

- Implement mechanisms for monitoring and evaluating the effectiveness of immigration policies. Regular assessments can help policymakers understand the impact of their initiatives and make necessary adjustments.

- Implement community policing strategies that build trust between law enforcement and immigrant communities. This can enhance public safety and foster cooperation in addressing immigration issues.

- Track down and prosecute the coyotes who make a profit by lying to immigrants about the risks and difficulties they could face as illegal aliens.

- Get the word out through social media and news outlets that the borders are not "open."

- The best thing the United States can do to help Central and South America is to stop "helping."

It's crucial to recognize that immigration is a complex issue with social, economic, and humanitarian dimensions. Effective solutions require a balanced and nuanced approach that considers the diverse factors influencing migration patterns. Policy changes should be informed by a commitment to fairness, justice, and the well-being of both immigrant and host communities.

We need to seek an effective way forward.

The Way Forward

In the complex tapestry of undocumented immigration, the threads of the challenges are tightly woven with the aspirations, struggles, and necessities of those seeking a better life beyond borders. It is a multifaceted issue, intricately linked to socio-economic disparities, political unrest, environmental changes, and a myriad of factors that drive individuals and families to embark on perilous journeys in search of safety and opportunity.

As we navigate the discourse surrounding undocumented immigration, it becomes evident that simplistic solutions fall short of addressing the root causes and intricacies involved. Walls and deterrent measures, while visible and tangible, often fail to grapple with the intangible forces compelling people to leave their homes. Comprehensive and sustainable solutions must recognize and account for the diverse factors that contribute to the very real conditions motivating migration.

In crafting effective responses, policymakers, advocates, and societies at large must acknowledge the economic disparities that drive individuals to seek better opportunities in foreign lands. Addressing these root causes involves fostering international collaboration, promoting economic development in regions of origin, and creating avenues for legal migration that align with the labor market needs of destination countries.

Political instability and persecution are catalysts for forced migration, and any comprehensive solution must incorporate diplomatic efforts to address these issues at their source. Encouraging dialogue, supporting human rights initiatives, and engaging with governments to create stable and inclusive societies are essential steps toward mitigating the desperation that fuels migration.

Moreover, the impact of environmental changes cannot be overlooked. Climate-induced displacement is a growing concern, and strategies must be devised to assist communities in adapting to changing conditions and building resilience. International cooperation on climate policies, coupled with humanitarian assistance, can contribute to minimizing displacement driven by environmental factors.

Recognizing the complexity of undocumented immigration requires us to approach the issue with empathy and a commitment to understanding the intricate web of interconnected challenges. It necessitates a departure from simplistic narratives and a move towards evidence-based, collaborative solutions that prioritize human dignity and the pursuit of a better life.

However, an expression attributed to Aristotle may be applied: "Excess is its own undoing." If bad solutions and ineffective measures are relied upon, the system will collapse of its own weight.

As we strive to untangle the intricate knot of undocumented immigration, let us remember that the path to resolution may seem dauntingly complex. However, it is in our shared humanity and commitment to addressing the root causes that we find the strength to weave a more just, compassionate, and equitable future for all those seeking refuge and opportunity beyond their borders.

To find the right answers, the right questions need to be asked. To find the right questions, we must see the bigger picture.

One thing is clear: simple solutions don't work.

References and Resources

To learn more about the complex issue of immigration, investigate the footnote links listed in each chapter as well as these books and publication resources:

- "U.S. Immigration Policy and Mexican/Central American Migration Flows: Then and Now" (Migration Policy Institute) - A comprehensive report providing an overview of historical and contemporary U.S. immigration policies and their impact on migration from Mexico and Central America.

- "U.S.-Mexico Economic Relations: Trends, Issues, and Implications" (Congressional Research Service)- A report analyzing economic relations between the U.S. and Mexico, including factors influencing migration patterns.

- "The U.S. Immigration Debate" (Council on Foreign Relations) - An interactive guide providing background information and perspectives on the U.S. immigration debate, including border security and policy challenges.

- "Migrant, Refugee, Smuggler, Savior" by Peter Tinti and Tuesday Reitano - Examines the role of smuggling networks in facilitating migration and provides insights into the challenges faced by migrants on their journey.

- "The Line Becomes a River: Dispatches from the Border" by Francisco Cantú - A memoir by a former Border Patrol agent, offering a personal perspective on the complexities and challenges of border enforcement.

- "Enrique's Journey" by Sonia Nazario - Follows the harrowing journey of a Honduran boy traveling to the U.S. to reunite with his mother, providing insight into the reasons behind migration.

- "American Dirt" by Jeanine Cummins - A novel that explores the experiences of a mother and son fleeing drug cartel violence in Mexico, shedding light on the dangers faced by migrants.

- "The Death and Life of Aida Hernandez: A Border Story" by Aaron Bobrow-Strain - Chronicles the life of Aida Hernandez, an undocumented immigrant, and explores the challenges faced by individuals navigating the U.S. immigration system.

- "Tell Me How It Ends: An Essay in 40 Questions" by Valeria Luiselli - Based on the author's experiences as a translator for unaccompanied migrant children, this book delves into the complexities of the immigration system.

These resources cover a range of perspectives and provide insights into the historical context, challenges, and potential solutions related to the southern border of the United States.

If you enjoyed this book, please take a few moments to write a nice review where you purchased it and recommend it to your friends and social media followers! TimTrottWrites.com/your-review

About the Author

Tim Trott is a writer who is passionate about investigating and shedding light on important issues. Whether fiction or non-fiction, his writing is characterized by a commitment to research and a keen ability to communicate complex topics with clarity, a skill honed during his early career in broadcasting.

A lifelong student and observer of current events and issues, Tim brings a wealth of perspective and insight to his work. While he may not be a widely known writer, the actual value of his writing lies in the information he provides and the quality of his communication. His writing is a testament to a lifetime spent in diverse occupations, each contributing to a tapestry of perspectives on the complex issues shaping our world.

Tim Trott's writing is informed by research; his exploration of this multifaceted topic goes beyond the headlines, delving into the nuances that often escape casual observation. Drawing on the skills cultivated throughout his career, Tim navigates the subject's complexities with a balanced and informed perspective.

Beyond the mere presentation of facts, Tim's writing reflects a commitment to fostering understanding and informed dialogue. His ability to distill intricate information into accessible narratives makes his work informative and engaging for readers from all walks of life.

In his post-retirement years, Tim Trott has found a renewed purpose in contributing to the discourse surrounding critical societal issues. Through his writing, he continues to share his wealth of knowledge, providing readers with the tools they need to form well-informed opinions on the pressing matters of our time.

Tim Trott invites you to visit his website at TimTrottWrites.com.

Please consider these other books by the author:

Biography: *Out of the Blue: The life and legend of Kirby "Sky King" Grant, First Through the Fire (Talbert Gray)*

Education: *Understanding WordPress 6.x for Beginners*

Security: *Guarding Against Online Identity Theft* and *Proteccion de Identidad*

Politics/History: *T is for Treason, Broken Border , Party of NO*

Science Fiction: *What If... (Vol 1)*

Misc/LCB: *LOTTO TRAKR*